ADVANCE PRAISE

"Donald Johnson offers up his unique insights through personal stories of triumph and failure — stories that are not only engaging to read but significant for anyone who wants to better understand Bay Street or how dedicated people can influence public policy."
—*Paul Martin, 21ˢᵗ Prime Minister of Canada*

"Don's efforts to remove capital gains tax on donations of listed securities have provided a permanent boost for charities and their ability to raise funds. His story is the perfect reminder that you can accomplish your goals if you put your mind to it and stick with it."
—*Jim Pattison, Founder, The Jim Pattison Group*

"This book is an honest assessment of Don's career and life lessons. The best line in the book, which any ex door-to-door salesman will recognize, is 'the sale starts when the customer says no.' It's a history lesson on what is required to be successful in building an investment bank."
—*Jack Cowin, Executive Chairman, Competitive Foods Australia*

"Don has forever changed the Canadian philanthropic landscape by successfully campaigning for tax reform. He continues to set a stellar example to others with all that he does to champion the transformative power of philanthropy in our country."
—*Karen Kain, Artistic Director, National Ballet of Canada*

"Despite having been the toast of Toronto's financial district, Donald Johnson always stayed true to his rural Manitoba values, which is perhaps why he remains so highly regarded as an investment strategist, a compassionate philanthropist, and a genuinely likable, well-rounded human being."
—*Hartley Richardson, President and CEO, James Richardson & Sons Ltd.*

"Don has seen everything, forgotten nothing, particularly the importance of giving back. A must-read for the best of finance."
—*Mark Carney, Former Governor, Bank of Canada and Bank of England*

LESSONS LEARNED ON BAY STREET

THE SALE BEGINS WHEN THE CUSTOMER SAYS *NO*

DONALD K. JOHNSON

BARLOW BOOKS
fine books for enterprising authors

Library and Archives Canada Cataloguing in Publication data available upon request.

ISBN 978-1-988025-46-9 (hardcover)

Printed in Canada

Publisher: Sarah Scott
Book producer: Tracy Bordian/At Large Editorial Services
Cover design: Paul Hodgson
Interior design and page layout: Liz Harasymczuk
Copy editing: Eleanor Gasparik
Proofreading: Joel Gladstone
Indexing: Wendy Thomas

For more information, visit **www.barlowbooks.com**

Barlow Book Publishing Inc.
96 Elm Avenue, Toronto, ON
Canada M4W 1P2

The final stages of this book were marked by great sadness. Anna, my loving companion since 1981 and wife of 30 years, passed away on August 15, 2020.

Anna was a force of nature and a lover of life, a successful entrepreneur, famed ballet teacher, consummate hostess, compassionate and generous friend — and much else besides. I'm honoured to dedicate this book to the woman whose support and encouragement contributed so much to my own success.

CONTENTS

A LIFETIME OF LESSONS

O n a warm and sunny day in France in the summer of 2019, I looked across the green grass of Vimy Ridge to the two towering limestone pillars of the Canadian National Vimy Memorial. I was spending quality time with my son, Carter, on a ten-day *Globe and Mail* cruise along the Seine from Paris to Normandy. As a regional director for an educational organization, Carter travels frequently for work so I don't get to see as much of him as I'd like to, and the cruise seemed like a great opportunity to catch up with his busy life.

When I thought about all the young lives that had been lost here—more than eleven thousand names of Canadians who died in the First World War in France are inscribed on the memorial's base—it drove home to me how lucky I am to have reached the age of eighty-four, to still be in good health, and to have enjoyed a long career in a field as varied and stimulating as investment banking.

I must confess, I do have some regrets about not spending enough time with my three children when they were young: I devoted a lot of time to my work, and along with striving to be financially independent, my biggest priority back then was (as it still is) to stay fit and healthy. It's very challenging to have the discipline to live a healthy lifestyle, and it takes a lot of time.

So, the truth is, my family was my third priority in the earlier years of my career. Fortunately, I have a good relationship with my kids now, and we often have a good laugh about those early days when our "quality time" consisted of going to the car wash, getting my hair cut, or spending Saturdays and Sundays at the office. On the Seine cruise, Carter and I joked that this was the most time I had spent with him in forty-five years—and he's forty-five years old.

But, humour aside, I am very grateful that I'm still around to enjoy my family. On top of that, I had a long and happy marriage with my second wife, Anna. I still get along well with my first wife and have a good relationship with my two stepsons. Also, I feel fortunate to be actively involved, through my philanthropic work, in helping some people who lead tougher lives than I do.

So, yes, things have turned out well in the end. And it's been a fascinating journey—one full of lessons.

That's why I'm writing this book: to share the lessons I've learned on Bay Street in the hope that readers, including those beyond Bay Street, can benefit from some of them—whether you're a university student trying to decide on a future career, a civic leader interested in philanthropy, a senior manager of a public company or a non-profit group who wants to make Canada a better place, an investment banker looking to make a big deal happen ... or anyone who may simply be interested in the keys to a long and satisfying life.

I'm a big fan of one-liners that have meaning. Friends, family, and business associates often hear me use borrowed words of wisdom such as these, which I call my rules of the road:

- The sale begins when the customer says *no*.
- Never put off until tomorrow what you can do today.
- Never give up.
- It's better to give it away with a warm hand than a cold hand.
- You learn a lot more from your failures than from your successes.
- Laughter is the best medicine.
- You're never too old to learn something new.

While some of these expressions may seem lighthearted, they have deep and genuine meaning, and that's what the lessons in this book try to highlight: how to choose the career that's right for you; the keys to achieving success in business; how to focus your time and energy so that you can make a real difference; how to approach philanthropy and experience the joy of giving back; what it takes to keep fit both mentally and physically; and the nuts and bolts of convincing governments to implement sound public policy. The list goes on. I hope you'll find at least some of these tips energizing and useful.

Because the best storytelling centres on real-life examples, this book shares some inside glimpses of the most exciting—and embarrassing—deals that I've had the good fortune to be involved in. These experiences have given me the opportunity to meet many fascinating people, from chief executives and board members to skilled health-care providers, and the wonderful people who dedicate their lives to helping society's most vulnerable.

Success in business demands initiative and perseverance—in other words, an entrepreneurial spirit. Former US President Calvin Coolidge put it this way: "Nothing in the world can take the place of persistence. Talent will not; nothing is more common than unsuccessful men with talent. Genius will not; unrewarded genius is almost a proverb. Education will not; the world is full of educated derelicts. Persistence and determination alone are omnipotent."[1]

In my case, the seeds of persistence were planted when I was a kid in small-town Manitoba, watching my dad come up with ways to make money and put food on the table, and then in my teenage years, seeing my mom take tough decisions and work her heart out so that I could go to university. My parents did what they had to in order to raise their four kids, and we reaped the benefits as we followed our own paths in life. I chose the business world, and I've loved every minute of it, especially the chance to work with a great group of people to help build Burns Fry into a blue-chip investment bank. The deals I've worked on have not just benefited our clients and our company but have also, I believe, helped propel key segments of Canada's economy.

There's no way I could have done all this if I hadn't enjoyed my work so much. Just think: according to a 2017 Gallup poll, only 15 per cent of employees worldwide are happy in their jobs.[2] That means 85 per cent are unhappy. It's so important to be in a job you love, and to make a change if you find you're in the wrong one. (It happened to me; you can read about it in Chapter 2.)

My visit to northern France with my son was a first for me, and I learned a lot more about First World War history than I'd known before. It just goes to show: you're never too old to learn something new. I hope the lessons I share in this book prove that to be true for you.

CHAPTER 1

BUFFETT TO THE RESCUE

Y ou have to hand it to Warren Buffett. Even at the age of eighty-six, the world's most famous investor was not only reading e-mails from octogenarians in Toronto but also wasting little time acting on them.

Take the message I sent him on the afternoon of Friday, June 9, 2017, asking whether he might be interested in discussing an investment in Home Capital Group, a Toronto mortgage lender struggling to stay afloat amid accusations that it had broken securities laws and that some of its mortgage brokers had falsi-fied loan applications. A run by depositors had brought Home Capital to the verge of collapse, and only an emergency infusion of cash could save it.

It occurred to me that the Sage of Omaha might be just the saviour Home Capital was looking for. After all, he had helped prop up both Goldman Sachs and Bank of America after the 2008 financial crisis, and the troubled Toronto lender fit many of his investment criteria.

What's more, I had nurtured a bond with Warren that stretched back twenty-three years. My long career has taught me that nothing is more valuable to investment bankers than their contacts book. Behind those business cards are the people who introduce us to the mergers and acquisitions (M&A), financings, and other deals that are the core of investment banking. They recommend us to their friends, their lawyers, and their business associates, ensuring that the deal machine keeps humming. In short, an investment banker's contacts drive his or her success—or failure. I have accumulated a mere 6,100 names in my contacts file, and one of those is Warren Buffett.

No sooner had the idea of Warren Buffett investing in Home Capital come to me than I e-mailed Brad Hardie, who was BMO Capital Markets' relationship manager for Home Capital, offering to find out whether Warren might be interested. Home Capital had retained BMO and RBC Capital Markets to help tackle its liquidity crisis and legal problems. Although I officially retired as a senior advisor to BMO in 2010, I still kept an office near the corner of King and Bay Streets, right next door to First Canadian Place, where the bank has its executive offices. That made it easy to stay in touch with former colleagues, and there's little I enjoy more than passing on ideas and contacts that might help those contacts to nail down a deal.

Following a meeting of the Home Capital board, Brad got back to me with word that the directors liked my idea. We realized the chances were slim that one of the world's legendary investors might be interested in rescuing a small and troubled lender in Canada. Even so, the directors wanted to be sure that they left no stone unturned in their struggle for survival. Brad agreed that I should reach out to Warren without delay.

My connection to Warren goes back to the mid-1990s when I was working on a big oil sands deal. At the time, I was a vice-chairman in Burns Fry's investment banking division, and one of my corporate clients was Sun Company, the oil and petrochemicals group now known as Sunoco. Sun's main interest in Canada was a 55 per cent stake in Suncor, which was already a sizable oil producer and would go on, as Suncor Energy, to become the biggest producer in the Alberta oil sands. In 1994, I was summoned to Sun's head office in Philadelphia to meet its chief executive, Robert Campbell, and chief financial officer, Bob Aiken. The two men told me that they were thinking of unloading Sun's stake in Suncor and were looking for advice on possible buyers, and how best to structure a deal. But there was a catch: I was not allowed to breathe a word about their intentions to Rick George, Suncor's chief executive, or any of his senior managers.

As any investment banker knows, a finely tuned process comes into play when a public company like Sun decides to sell a major asset. Having been engaged to explore the alternatives, our job was to advise Sun on the pros and cons of selling either directly to another company or selling the shares through the stock market. One of the first steps is to prepare a confidentiality agreement that prospective buyers must sign before they can receive details of the acquisition opportunity. Without that, we could not even disclose the name of the company. Even after the confidentiality agreement was in place, the only material on Suncor that we could provide was information already in the public realm. Supplying non-public information to a bidder would require a go-ahead from Suncor management in Calgary. Of course, that was out of the question given that their bosses in Philadelphia had forbidden me from disclosing a word to them about the parent company's plans.

Suncor was already a jewel of a company in the mid-1990s, yet finding a buyer proved a bigger challenge than we expected. Although most people thought of Suncor as an oil producer, its operations around Fort McMurray were more akin to open-pit mines, and concern about their impact on the environment was growing. We quickly identified several global energy companies as potential buyers. But as soon as we mentioned the name Suncor, they backed away because they were not familiar or comfortable with mining technology. On the other side of the coin, the big mining companies that we approached saw Suncor as an energy play, and also ran the other way. But there was one exception—Toronto's American Barrick (now Barrick Gold).

At the time, American Barrick was moving into the top ranks of the world's gold producers. Peter Munk, the company's founder and chairman, also had a foot in the energy industry through Barrick's holding company, Horsham Corporation, which owned oil refineries and a chain of Midwest gas stations. With this in mind, I contacted Peter. We had met once or twice socially, thanks to an introduction through my wife Anna, but had never done business together. Within a few days, Peter, his chief financial officer, Greg Wilkins, and I boarded Barrick's corporate jet for the short flight to Philadelphia. Peter was sufficiently tempted by the idea of buying Sun's stake in Suncor that he asked Barrick's president, Bob Smith, to fly to Fort McMurray and check out Suncor's oil sands operations. Suncor wasn't aware of his visit, of course; Bob rented a helicopter and flew over the oil sands, getting a first-hand view of the vast tailings ponds that contained the waste from Suncor's bitumen-mining operations. Bob's gruff demeanour masked a razor-sharp mind, and he returned from Alberta firmly of the opinion that Barrick should take a pass. The environmental risks and costs posed by the tailings ponds were too great, he concluded. To his credit, Bob had the foresight to identify these risks, which would later become an enormous challenge for the oil sands industry.

Barrick's withdrawal left us with few options. I had scoured the world's major energy and mining companies for buyers, with little to show for my efforts. But as has often happened in the course of my career, a bolt of inspiration saved me. As I once again ran through all the possibilities, the name Warren Buffett suddenly came to mind.

I had followed Warren's career closely, read numerous articles about him, and paid close attention to his wise investment strategy, even applying it to my personal portfolio. What especially impressed me was that he didn't invest for short-term success, but instead took big bets on a relatively small number of companies that he would hold on to not for months or years, but for decades. And he had a really strong management team. He was obviously doing something right. It was also clear to me that Suncor fit several of his much-publicized criteria for a sound investment. It had a dominant position in its industry, with a track record stretching back several years, plus excellent long-term growth potential and the benefits of being in a sector with high barriers to entry.

I quickly fired off a special-delivery letter to Omaha. Most other investment bankers might have picked up the phone and called, but I carefully drafted a letter outlining a unique opportunity that, in my opinion, met many of the Buffett investment criteria. The approach got his attention. It didn't take long for him to get back to me, and we agreed to meet at his office immediately after the forthcoming annual general meeting of Berkshire Hathaway, his listed holding company.

My overriding memory of our first get-together was Warren's sharp mind and equally sharp sense of humour. We met in his modest office and I sat opposite him as he sat at his desk. We each drank a bottle of Coca-Cola. It was the same modest office he'd had for over twenty-five years. Before I left, a photographer took our picture; it hangs in my office to this day, labelled "The Sage of Omaha."

Warren and his colleagues followed up with numerous questions as part of the due diligence process. They eventually indicated that they would indeed be interested in the Suncor control stake. But there was one big stumbling block. The price that Berkshire proposed was about 15 per cent below Suncor's market value, an unusually generous discount for a company with such a strong market position and bright future. We were reluctant to recommend such a low price to Sun, and instead went to work on other alternatives.

My colleagues at Burns Fry were confident that we could get a better deal by selling Sun's shares through the stock market. However, the Americans wanted to be sure that they could offload their shares at a satisfactory price and that the market wouldn't move against them, cutting into their proceeds. That left us with no choice but to structure the sale as a "bought deal," where we would buy all the Suncor shares at a pre-set price, form a syndicate with other investment dealers, and then sell the shares to our various institutional and retail clients. Given Suncor's size, our director of equity capital markets, Brent Fullard, recommended that we split the transaction into three instalments.

The deal finally closed in June 1995 at a discount of just 5 per cent below Suncor's market price, a far better result for Sun than Berkshire Hathaway had proposed. Sun ended up receiving a hefty $1.1 billion for its shares, but I wonder to this day whether Robert Campbell and his colleagues wished that they had hung on to their Canadian jewel. Suncor went on to much bigger and better things. Thanks to Rick George's strong leadership, growing investor interest in the Alberta oil sands, and a string of acquisitions, especially of Petro-Canada in 2009, the Calgary company now has a market value of more than $50 billion.

Bay Street may have turned Warren Buffett down on Suncor, but it had definitely not turned its back on him. There were no hard feelings; in fact, I made a point of staying in touch, and Warren invited me to attend several of Berkshire Hathaway's legendary annual meetings in Omaha. I had never realized that I could learn so much and have so much fun at a corporate annual meeting. These are huge affairs, held in a cavernous 18,000-seat arena in Omaha. The conversations between Warren and his long-time partner Charlie Munger are especially informative and entertaining, with lots of humorous exchanges and lively banter.

Of course, I also wanted to be sure that if Warren ever did end up doing a deal in Canada, my firm would have the bragging rights of having brought it to his attention. Burns Fry went through a massive transformation in 1994, when Bank of Montreal acquired and merged it with Nesbitt Thomson, the bank's own investment dealing arm, and renamed the combined—and much bigger—entity BMO Nesbitt Burns.

So it was under a new letterhead that I reached out to Warren again in November 2002 to gauge his interest in Royal and Sun Alliance Insurance Company (R&SA) of Canada, the country's fourth-largest property and casualty insurer. R&SA Canada's British parent, Royal and Sun Alliance Insurance Group PLC, was going through a rough patch, and we figured that it could raise some badly needed cash by selling its Canadian arm. Again, Warren was quick to get back to me, but this time the answer was a definite "no." He didn't give a reason, and I never pressed him for one.

Our next encounter came five years later in October 2007. I learned that Warren was due to speak at a high-powered reception and dinner at the Royal Ontario Museum to raise funds for the Toronto General & Western Hospital Foundation. I was (and still am) a director of the foundation, so I dropped him a note a few weeks before the event, saying how much I was looking forward to seeing him again, and perhaps discussing another attractive deal in Canada. Sure enough, we found time for a congenial chat over pre-dinner drinks, and then again afterwards. I followed up with a suggestion that Berkshire Hathaway consider an investment in Canadian Pacific Railway (CP Rail), Canada's oldest railroad company. It seemed right up Warren's street, given that he already owned stakes in three US railroads. Alas, he replied that CP Rail did not meet his investment criteria. Too bad, because five years later, another well-known US investor, Bill Ackman, won a bruising battle for control of CP. Its share price has more than tripled since then.

Warren was on my mind yet again as my family and I prepared to celebrate my eightieth birthday on June 18, 2015. To mark the occasion, my wife, Anna, organized a party in our garden, and we invited 250 friends to join us for what we hoped would be an evening for all to remember. We spent many hours pondering the choice of entertainment. Ideally, we wanted a singer, preferably a Canadian, who was popular in the 1970s and 1980s. Our research eventually led to Paul Anka, who had long been one of my favourite singers and had wowed us at Ted Rogers's seventy-fifth birthday party a few years earlier. Paul grew up in Ottawa, and besides his own blockbuster hits like "Diana" and "Put Your Head on My Shoulder," he also wrote "My Way" for Frank Sinatra. Sure enough, he was available for my party and put on a terrific show for us. We didn't get to bed until after midnight, and I was inundated over the next few days with complimentary e-mails and phone calls.

Knowing that Warren Buffett was a keen Paul Anka fan, we invited him to the party. Unfortunately, he couldn't attend, but I took the liberty of sending him a CD of the performance. A few weeks later, a letter arrived in the mail:

> *Dear Don,*
> *Many thanks for sending me the items from your 80th. I especially appreciated the Paul Anka CD—you really hit the spot there.*
> *Best wishes.*
> *Sincerely,*
> *Warren E. Buffett*[3]

With a compliment like that, I would not easily forget Warren Buffett. Nor, I figured, would he likely forget me. And so it happened that, two years later, our stars finally aligned.

Home Capital's troubles came to a head in April 2017, when the Ontario Securities Commission (OSC) announced that it would lay charges against the company's senior managers and directors for failing to disclose that some of their brokers had falsified information on mortgage applications. A couple of US hedge funds, smelling blood, had taken large short positions in Home Capital stock in anticipation of a steep fall in the share price. They saw the OSC's allegations as a heaven-sent opportunity to draw attention to the company's woes on LinkedIn, Twitter, and other social media. The publicity also quickly undermined the confidence of individual investors. Frightened depositors, who had financed a significant chunk of Home Capital's mortgage portfolio, headed for the exits, withdrawing more than $1.6 billion in the course of a few weeks. By mid-May, the company had lost 94 per cent of its savings deposits, and its share price had nosedived from $25 to $6. Its troubles were even starting to raise questions about the stability of other Canadian financial institutions.

Keeping the ship afloat became the most urgent priority. The board managed to come up with a temporary fix by arranging an emergency $2-billion loan from the Healthcare of Ontario Pension Plan. Fortunately, the bailout could be arranged quickly because each side knew the other well. The pension fund's chief executive, Jim Keohane, was a Home Capital director, while Kevin Smith, Home Capital's chairman, was serving on the fund's board. Even so, the company's dire situation meant that it had little choice but to pay a hefty 10 per cent interest rate, plus a non-refundable commitment fee of $100 million. It clearly needed to find a more sustainable solution—and fast—to ensure survival.

Here was another opportunity that seemed to tick several of Warren Buffett's boxes. A cornerstone of his investment philosophy is that the best time to buy is when everyone else is heading for the exits. That is especially true when a company is a leader in its field, when there are significant barriers to entry, and when it has a proven track record of performance over many years. All those criteria applied in spades to Home Capital.

Having been given the green light by BMO Capital Markets, I fired off an e-mail to Debbie Bosanek, Warren's executive assistant—Warren himself doesn't use e-mail—on the afternoon of Friday, June 9.

Dear Warren,

Just to refresh your memory, we first met about twenty-three years ago to discuss the potential opportunity to acquire 55 per cent of Suncor Energy from Sun Company in Philadelphia...[4]

I went on to remind him of our various encounters, from our first meeting in 1994, when we were looking for a buyer for Suncor, to our chat at the Royal Ontario Museum thirteen years later. I included two attachments that I thought would help grab his attention: a copy of the letter that I wrote after the Royal Ontario Museum event mentioning CP Rail, and a photo of the two of us at one of the Berkshire Hathaway annual meetings that I had attended in Omaha. I then got to the point:

I thought you might be interested in having a look at another attractive Canadian investment opportunity— Home Capital. As you know, crises create opportunities and the best time to consider an investment is when no one else wants to buy.[5]

I asked Debbie to bring the matter to Warren's attention as soon as possible. Three days later, at noon on Monday, June 12, I followed up with a second e-mail specifically proposing that Warren consider becoming the largest shareholder in Home Capital. The best way to do that, I suggested, would be to make a significant investment in a private placement of shares and put up $2 billion in loans to replace the Healthcare of Ontario Pension Plan financing:

Such an investment would restore confidence in the future of the company and result in a dramatic increase in the share price. The benefit of such an alternative would be an attractive return for both Berkshire Hathaway and current shareholders.[6]

As usual, it didn't take long for Berkshire Hathaway to spring into action. Ted Weschler, one of Warren's top investment managers, called Brad Hardie at BMO on the same day that I sent my second e-mail. They spoke for two hours, and two days later, on Wednesday, June 14, Ted landed in Toronto to meet Home Capital's board, senior management, and financial advisors. They met again the next day, and the meeting ended with Ted making an offer to buy 40 million Home Capital shares at an average price of $10 apiece and provide a new $2-billion credit facility. The shares were trading below $12 at the time, and the $10 offer price seemed a reasonable discount. Everyone around the table quickly agreed to his proposal.

We crossed another big hurdle right around that time when Home Capital reached a settlement with the Ontario Securities Commission over the regulator's allegations of wrongdoing. News of the settlement pushed the shares back up to $14. BMO and RBC tried to persuade Ted and his colleagues at Berkshire to raise the bid price but, understandably, they would have none of it. All was set for the public announcement.

At 11 p.m. on June 21, the news release came through that Berkshire Hathaway was investing in an issue of Home Capital common shares at $9.55 each to acquire a 19.9 per cent equity stake, as well as lending it $2 billion at an interest rate of 9.5 per cent. Provided Home Capital shareholders agreed, Berkshire would also invest in a second tranche of equity in September 2017, taking its ownership to 38.4 per cent.

The TSX said Berkshire could not buy more than 20 per cent of Home Capital without shareholder approval, and a special shareholder meeting was scheduled for September to approve the second tranche.

The news put a rocket under Home Capital's shares, propelling them up to $19 when markets opened the next morning. In other words, Berkshire had almost doubled its money overnight. More than that, its investment would benefit everyone else involved in the Home Capital saga—other shareholders, customers, depositors, management, employees, and directors as well as the financial advisors.

Regrettably, the shareholders voted a month and a half later to reject Warren's second investment, which would have almost doubled his stake. However, Berkshire remained Home Capital's biggest shareholder until late 2018 and had the satisfaction of not only making a substantial profit on its original investment but also knowing that it had played a vital role in reviving an important business that was close to death's door. As for myself, my reward was the warm feeling that comes from knowing that I had played a modest part in pulling together one of the most momentous deals in the recent history of Canada's financial services industry.

On July 17, less than a month after the deal closed, another e-mail arrived from Omaha:

> *Dear Don,*
> *Well you didn't know what you were going to start when you sent me that e-mail a month or so ago.*

Paul and I are going to appear together at the NFL Hall of Fame dinner in a month. We better keep those big guys happy with our performance—so I'll let Paul do 99 per cent of the singing.

On August 30, I'll let you know how age 87 is.

Best regards,

Warren[7]

And yet another on August 10:

Hi Don,

Just a note to let you know that last week Paul and I sang together at the NFL Annual Hall of Fame dinner in Canton, Ohio. You can see this on Paul's Facebook page. (I've never had a Facebook account myself but someone else showed me.)

I think the Home Capital transaction had societal benefit to Canada, and I'm glad for that. It wouldn't have happened, of course, without you.

Best regards,

Warren[8]

As I took in these messages, I reflected on the down-to-earth lessons that I learned from Warren Buffett in the twenty-three years since we first met. I expand on those lessons later in this book. Above all, I was touched, as many others have been, by Warren's modesty. A Paul Anka CD clearly meant as much to one of the world's richest and most famous men as a billion-dollar deal.

CHAPTER 2

FROM LUNDAR TO BAY STREET

Whenever I go back to Lundar, Manitoba, where I was born, I can't help but think about my Icelandic grandparents and the other pioneers who made such a huge contribution to opening up this remote part of Canada. Lundar is located about 60 miles north of Winnipeg, near the eastern shore of Lake Manitoba. It traces its Icelandic roots back to 1887, when John Sigfusson, its first homesteader, arrived there.

Icelanders had several good reasons to make a fresh start across the Atlantic Ocean in the late nineteenth century. Apart from the challenges of surviving long, cold winters in their home country, many had become unsettled by one of the largest volcanic eruptions in Iceland's history, in 1875. The eruption, followed by many smaller ones over the next few months, left the eastern side of the island covered in a heavy ash. What's more, a growing population was straining resources in many communities. Almost twenty thousand Icelanders, many of them farmers and fishermen, emigrated to North America between 1874 and 1914. Manitoba's rich farmland and two large lakes, Lake Manitoba and Lake Winnipeg, made that part of the world especially attractive to them. The town of Gimli, not far from Lundar, is still said to have the largest Icelandic community outside of Iceland.

The original settlers in Manitoba's Interlake region made their living from dairy and cattle farming, and from fishing on Lake Manitoba. One newcomer opened a post office in 1890, naming it Lundi—Icelandic for meadow—after the farm in Iceland where his wife had been raised. According to the history books, a bureaucratic mix-up in Ottawa turned Lundi into Lundar.

My grandparents, on both sides of the family, were among the first group of Icelanders to settle in the area. My father's parents, Björn Jónsson and Guðrún Pálsdóttir, took a boat from Iceland to Scotland, and another to Quebec City, then travelled west by train to Winnipeg. They had eight children at the time, one of whom was my father, Páll Björnsson, who was born in 1884 and so was a small boy when they settled in Lundar in 1888. Not long after arriving, my father and his siblings, like many other European immigrants, changed their surname, figuring that Johnson would make them more socially acceptable among the locals. Meanwhile, my maternal grandparents, Magnús Kristjánsson and Margrét Daníelsdóttir, who were from western Iceland, had settled in the hamlet of Otto, a short drive east of Lundar, where my mother was born in 1901.

I was born on June 18, 1935, the second youngest of my parents' four children—the eldest was Margret, next was Paul, and Cyril (Cy) was the youngest. As you'd expect for people of Icelandic heritage, all of us were fair-haired and blue-eyed. We had a simple but happy childhood. Our bungalow was just 600 square feet in size, and had no basement. There were two bedrooms—one for my parents and the other shared by all four kids. We had no electricity (Lundar didn't get it until I was a teenager) or running water; the bathroom was an outhouse in the backyard, and getting there was no fun for at least seven months of the year, when northern Manitoba was gripped by frigid temperatures and snow. We relied on the wood stove in the centre of the house to keep us warm; it had to be constantly fed during winter. We didn't have a refrigerator, so to prevent food from spoiling, my parents dug a deep hole outside and placed a container in it for storing perishables. Wooden boards covered the hole to prevent us kids from falling in, and to keep animals out.

Although we didn't have much money, my mother was generous and would often welcome people in need into our home for a meal. She was well respected in Lundar, and very industrious. On top of all the work of running the household and tending to our cows and the vegetable garden, she earned some extra cash by making socks and mitts on a little knitting machine and selling them to townspeople and to the fishermen who worked on Lake Manitoba. Every Christmas, our parents gave us each just one gift, and it was always the same: long underwear!

My father Páll was an entrepreneur. That was a good thing because the Great Depression hit Lundar hard, and money was scarce. For a time, he ran a custom hay-baling operation, and my mother helped with the labour. Since my brother Cy was too young to attend school at that time, they'd take him along. My mother would build him a "house" out of hay bales to keep him protected from the wind and cold while they worked.

My father also started a livery stable and a company called Lundar Transport, which picked up groceries, building materials, and other merchandise from Winnipeg and delivered them to local stores. And he bought horses at auctions in Winnipeg, transported them to Lundar, and sold them to local farmers.

My dad roped the rest of us into the family business, too. We owned three cows that my mother milked twice a day. Margret, Paul, Cy, and I delivered the bottled milk to our village neighbours at a price of 10 cents a bottle. Paul, besides a Friday job delivering mail to a nearby hamlet—snuggled under blankets on a horse-drawn sleigh in winters—had the job of taking the cows back to their pasture each evening, about a half-mile from the house.

My classmates and I probably spent more time at the Lundar Pool Room, a bar with pool tables, than our parents would have liked. To this day, my brothers still talk about how good I became at shooting pool. We also watched almost every game in the Interlake baseball and hockey leagues, and played endless card games with family and friends. And we'd spend hours in the empty lot next to our house playing Kick the Can. You made your own fun back then.

Some of the happiest years of my childhood were at Lundar Primary School. Memories of my school days came flooding back in 1995 when Margret called to tell me that Lundar was planning a big celebration to mark the 100th birthday of the town's oldest resident, Pauline Johnson (no relation). Pauline had been one of our favourite teachers at Lundar Primary, and Margret thought it would be a good idea for all four of us Johnson siblings to attend her birthday party. The first question that came to my mind was: what on earth can I give my former teacher for her 100th birthday? With the help of friends in Lundar, I learned that the community had been trying to raise money for almost fifteen years to build a library. The municipality had donated a piece of land, but $50,000 was still needed for the building. Margret, Paul, Cy, and I decided to contribute $25,000 on a dollar-for-dollar matching basis to donations for the balance. We decided to announce our gift at the birthday party and to suggest that the library be named after Pauline.

I will always remember my conversation with Pauline as she welcomed guests to her birthday party at the Lundar Community Hall. "Ms. Johnson, you probably don't remember me," I started off. "You taught me in grade one." Bright as a button, she jabbed her finger at me: "I taught you in grade one *and* in grade two!" Less than three years later, on July 11, 1998, I had the pleasure of cutting the ribbon at the official opening of the Pauline Johnson Library, with my former teacher by my side. By then, she was a sprightly one hundred and two.

At the ribbon-cutting ceremony, I announced that I would donate another $25,000 to the library for furnishings and equipment. Libraries are so important to the vibrancy of a town and the education of its residents. I was happy to do my part.

The simple but contented routines of our childhood were sadly interrupted when my dad developed Alzheimer's disease in the late 1940s, while I was still a young teenager. Not long after, we had little choice but to admit him to a hospital in Selkirk, more than an hour's drive away. He died in 1953.

As I entered my teens, our family was starting to broaden its horizons. Around the time that my dad was admitted to hospital, Margret and Paul moved to Winnipeg to pursue their careers. Margret became a hairdresser, and Paul initially worked for the Eaton's department store. In 1959, he started his own business, Certified Carpet Cleaners (it has been going strong ever since and is now owned by his son, my nephew Rodney). Meanwhile, Cy and I were still in school, so we remained with our mother in Lundar.

After I completed my junior matriculation year, my mother was adamant that I should plan to attend university. However, I needed a senior certificate to apply, and the local school offered only junior. I'd have to study in Winnipeg, but we couldn't afford for me to go to boarding school. The only option was for all of us to make the move to the big city. Many of my mother's friends in Lundar tried to discourage her from taking such a step into the unknown, but she was a force of nature and wouldn't be dissuaded. It was that important to her that I continue my education. My brothers always said I was the brains of the family, and while I didn't necessarily agree with them, my mother's decision to move us from Lundar to Winnipeg so that I could attend university changed my life.

So, in 1952, we sold our little house in Lundar, and my mother, Cy, and I made Winnipeg our new home. We rented the second floor of a house on Lipton Street, in a family neighbourhood west of downtown. Soon, Margret and Paul, both employed, moved in with us. It was a two-bedroom suite: mother's bedroom became my study in the daytime; my brothers and I slept in the other bedroom; and Margret had a cot set up in the kitchen. To keep us fed, my mother continued knitting socks and mitts that she sold to Lake Manitoba fishermen, and she also worked for a time in a nearby laundromat. Eventually, she got a full-time job working the lunch counter at the Kresge store on Portage Avenue downtown.

Coming to the big city was certainly an adjustment, but I made friends quite quickly. One good friend from school, Bill, lived across the road. Plus, I played a little hockey, so I met many other boys that way, too. I graduated in 1953, with a senior matriculation certificate from Daniel McIntyre Collegiate

Institute. Although I spent only a year at DMCI, I am still in touch with several of the friends I made there.

Meantime, Cy joined the Royal Bank of Canada as a teller and utility clerk, and spent his career moving up through the ranks. Thanks to an RBC scholarship program, he later graduated with a Bachelor of Commerce degree from the University of Manitoba, and then worked in Calgary, Edmonton, and Denver, Colorado, in increasingly senior management positions. He retired in 1994 and now lives in Canmore, Alberta.

I had no idea when I matriculated what I wanted to do with my life, but decided to apply to the University of Manitoba's engineering school for no better reason than my strongest marks in high school were in math, physics, and chemistry.

University was a real eye-opener for a lad from Lundar. The people I met were interesting to me both academically and socially; because many were from Winnipeg, I was exposed to a wider world. As I recall, there were no women in our class, but I did get to meet some girls from other faculties. But besides occasionally going to the movies downtown and to some dances— Louis Armstrong's music was popular then—I didn't do a lot of dating. Sometimes I helped fellow students with their homework at our flat on Lipton Street, and I did continue to play pool, even earning a little pocket change from it. Plus, to help pay for my tuition, I managed to find labourer jobs for two whole summers with the Canadian National Railway, helping to maintain the tracks.

After completing two years at U of M, I decided to specialize in electrical engineering because I figured it had the best career potential. I began looking for full-time work even before I graduated in 1957, but it was much tougher going than expected. The only openings for electrical engineers in Manitoba at that time were with Manitoba Telephone System and the Manitoba Power Commission (now Manitoba Hydro), both provincial government agencies. The last thing I wanted was to work for a government bureaucracy, so I decided to widen my job search to other parts of the country.

That led me to a one-year electronics training program at Canadian General Electric (CGE), a subsidiary of the giant US industrial conglomerate better known by its initials, GE. The fact that the opening was in Toronto made it even more appealing. I had never been to Ontario before and was excited at the thought of spending at least a few years in an even bigger city than Winnipeg.

I fell in love with Toronto from the moment I arrived. It didn't take long to discover that the theatres, art galleries, restaurants, and universities were unlike anything I had experienced in Manitoba. But job one was to find a place to live. My first home was a small rental apartment on Dufferin Street about a fifteen-minute walk from the CGE plant where I was to start my training.

My new work environment was also a real tonic. One of my first impressions at CGE was the thrill of meeting other newly minted electrical engineers from across Canada. The training program itself offered everything that I had hoped for, and more. We spent the year rotating through six different divisions, with two months in each. Some, such as marketing, finance, and administration, were far removed from engineering, and they opened my eyes for the first time to the real world of business.

My first two-month assignment was in marketing, where I was lucky enough to work for Bob Gillespie. Bob, who had emigrated from Scotland in the 1950s, became a valued mentor and gave me great advice on my future career options. I felt comfortable going into his office and saying, "Look, I'm having an issue with such-and-such. What do you suggest?" He was a good listener, and I trusted his advice. He went on to become CGE's chief executive and to be involved in many philanthropic pursuits. He remains a good friend to this day.

At the end of the training year, we were eligible to apply for a permanent job in the area that we liked best. I was not at all sure that I wanted to pursue a career in engineering, so I jumped at the opportunity to try some of the other options. Thanks in no small measure to Bob Gillespie, the two assignments I enjoyed most were marketing and finance, and my mind was soon set on a job in one of those divisions. But then matters took an unexpected turn. The economy sank into recession in 1958, and CGE laid off ten of the thirteen engineers who had enrolled in the training program. I was lucky enough to be one of the three survivors, but the not-so-good news was that, whether I liked it or not, the only job available if I wanted to stay on at General Electric was in design engineering.

If nothing else, the year I spent designing television sets and radar transmitters made me realize once and for all that I was not cut out to be an engineer. But while design engineering may not have provided much job satisfaction, it still left open the question: if not engineering, then what? Marketing and finance had definitely become my prime interests, but I was not at all sure how a junior electrical engineer would find a marketing or finance job.

The solution began to unfold one day in 1959, when I happened to spot a job ad from Federal Electric, a subsidiary of ITT, the US company that was emerging at that time as the model of a multinational conglomerate. Federal Electric had the contract to operate and maintain the Distant Early Warning Line, popularly known as the DEW Line, a string of radar stations across the Canadian Arctic designed to alert the US military to Russian bombers that might try to infiltrate North American air space. The company was looking for radar technicians to maintain the stations—and offering some juicy carrots: a salary three times higher than I was making as a junior engineer in Toronto, plus free food and accommodation. There was just one snag: it would mean moving to Cambridge Bay, a hamlet with a population of one thousand on Victoria Island, about 185 miles north of the Arctic Circle in what is now Nunavut.

Since I was still paying off student loans, I figured that giving up the easy life in Toronto was a small sacrifice for the huge jump in earnings. So I applied for the job, and by the summer of 1959, I was on a turbo prop plane making the long journey north.

Living and working in Cambridge Bay was a big adjustment, in more ways than one. The DEW Line staff all stayed in a large, barracks-like building. We each had our own bedroom, but had to share bathrooms and dining facilities. When I wasn't working, I spent my time reading, taking long walks, and photographing the breathtaking Arctic scenery. My fellow technicians were great company, especially during the long, dark winters. I also had my first encounters with Canada's Inuit people, who gave me a glimpse into their fascinating history and culture. All in all, I enjoyed my time in the Far North, though I certainly missed Toronto—the restaurants, the arts scene, movie theatres, cultural amenities, and diverse population that only a big city can offer.

I had been in the Arctic only a few months when I was promoted to station manager, with a hefty salary increase. At the age of just twenty-four, I had landed my first management job.

This was a big step forward because it took me away from the day-to-day grind of nitty-gritty technical work and exposed me to some of the broader issues, such as personnel and financial management, that were of far more interest to me. Not long after my promotion, I met another manager, who had recently graduated from the University of Western Ontario (now Western University), and we had a long talk about my interest in marketing and finance. I was looking for some advice on how to find a job in these fields after I returned to Toronto. He had graduated with an MBA degree and convinced me that the best way to pursue a marketing or finance career was to follow the same route.

But the MBA plan had to be put on hold for a year after I received yet another promotion, this time with responsibility for several radar stations stretching across the Arctic. The perks were just too tempting to turn it down. Not only did the promotion come with a raise but also Federal Electric offered me a substantial bonus if I was willing to stay in Cambridge Bay for another year.

At that time, only four universities in Canada offered MBA courses—the University of Toronto, the University of British Columbia, Queen's University, in Kingston, and the University of Western Ontario, in London. I set my mind on Western and in early 1961, as my extra year up north was nearing an end, I applied to the business school with a view to starting my studies that September. Trouble was, if I left my job in the early fall, I would not qualify for the special contract bonus. Thankfully, Federal Electric agreed to extend my contract from September 1961 to June 1962 so that I could complete the first year of the MBA, and then return to the DEW Line in the spring of 1962 to work off the remaining two months of my contract.

All went smoothly, and by the spring of 1963 I could proudly write the letters *MBA* after my name. About one hundred of us graduated that year, but not a single one was a woman. By contrast, of the 144 Western MBA graduates in 2018, 36—or a quarter of the total—were women. Many of my MBA classmates at Western became very good friends, none more so than David Jon Thomson, whose grandfather also came from Iceland and who worked for former prime minister Pierre Trudeau before making a career with Oxford Development Group and Great-West Life Insurance. David has arranged several class reunions, always fun events. Most recently we had our fifty-five-year get-together in the fall of 2018.

Another of my Western classmates, Joe Murphy, hit the jackpot with a summer job at Burns Bros. and Denton, one of Canada's most highly regarded brokerage firms. When we got together at the start of our second year, Joe whetted my appetite for Bay Street with stories about the firm's partners and the many interesting executives, bureaucrats, and investors whom he had encountered over the summer.

The die was cast. Investment banking sounded right up my alley, and I was champing at the bit to get started. I sent out application letters in the spring of 1963, and several firms called me in for interviews. Joe was kind enough to introduce me to the key partners at Burns Bros., including Charles Burns, the co-founder; his nephew Latham Burns; Peter Eby; Don Boxer; and Tim Beatty, who was president at the time.

Sure enough, I received an offer not long afterwards to join the firm as a securities analyst in the research department. I could not have been happier. Everything I had heard about the culture at Burns Bros. resonated with me, especially the emphasis that the partners placed on putting customers and employees ahead of their own personal interests. They also seemed to go out of their way to share the credit for their successes. All in all, I was confident that Burns Bros. and I would be a perfect fit. So at the age of twenty-seven, I was all set to make Bay Street my second home.

Some quick decisions were needed. Within a week or two, I had moved into a new apartment at 135 Lawton Boulevard, close to Yonge and Davisville, and had invited two of my former classmates—Bud McMorran and Larry Organ—to join me as roommates. A new suit and a couple of white shirts followed. My mother told me how happy she was with the direction my life was taking. On June 3, 1963, I walked into the Burns Bros. offices in the Bank of Nova Scotia building on the northeast corner of King Street and Bay Street, ready to start what would turn out to be a long and most satisfying career.

The fifty-seven years that followed have certainly been an extraordinary blessing. I rose through the ranks of Burns Bros. as it morphed into Burns Fry, then Nesbitt Burns, and—now—BMO Capital Markets. I have had the opportunity to travel the world and meet the CEOs and senior executives of some major North American, European, African, and Asian companies. Along the way, I have had the good fortune of being involved in some of corporate Canada's most exciting and challenging deals, and the privilege of working with many wonderful colleagues.

Even so, I've taken care not to lose touch with my roots. For many of us, the place where we were born fades over the years into little more than a name that we enter on a passport application. In my case, however, it has been a real pleasure to maintain a lifelong affection for both Iceland and Lundar, Manitoba. My siblings and I visited the land of our forebears for the first time in 1987. Our stay in Iceland was both a moving and uplifting experience. We visited the places where our grandparents were born, and we hired a tour guide to show us the mountains, geysers, and other spectacular scenery that the island has to offer. I've subsequently visited Iceland another five times—once for a family reunion, and three times in pursuit of a business opportunity. I am hoping there will be many more occasions, especially now that there are direct flights between Toronto and Reykjavík.

As for Lundar, with a current population of just 1,300, it has not grown or changed much over the years, although the house we grew up in was demolished a few years ago, when neighbours bought the property and wanted to make more room for their growing family. But it remains a vibrant, hard-working community that continues to honour its Icelandic roots.

My siblings and I have often returned there over the years. One sad occasion was in 1980 for my mother Fjóla's funeral. She spent the rest of her life in Winnipeg, moving from our first home at 933 Lipton Street to a house on Home Street that Cy bought and where they lived together for a number of years. After Cy moved to Calgary in 1966, my mother stayed in the house until the mid-1970s, when she moved to the Lions Manor seniors residence and, then, toward the end of her life, to a long-term care home where she died of a heart attack. We had a family visitation in Winnipeg, followed the next day by a funeral service at the picturesque Lutheran church on First Avenue in Lundar. She was buried next to our father in the Lundar cemetery.

I owe so much to Lundar, and I've always thought it important to give something back to the community. In 1987, the same year as our first trip to Iceland, my siblings and I returned to Lundar to celebrate the 100th anniversary of the town's founding.

It was a really heart-warming experience to reconnect with many of our relatives, former classmates, neighbours, and friends. To mark the centenary, I set up a scholarship, dedicated to the memory of our mother, for the top graduating student from Lundar School to continue with his or her post-secondary education. I also set up a fund in 2010 for the Coldwell Community Foundation, designed to improve the quality of life in the rural municipality of Coldwell, where Lundar is located. My hope is that this kind of giving will encourage others who have had success in their careers to support the communities that made it all possible.

We still return to Lundar every summer. At the end of each July, the Icelandic community in nearby Gimli hosts the Icelandic Festival of Manitoba, known as Islendingadagurinn. For many years the festival gave Margret, Paul, Cy, and me the perfect excuse to visit Lundar and to host a lunch at the Pauline Johnson Library. The event has been a highlight of each year, a great opportunity not only to see my siblings but also to catch up with other family members and the many residents of Lundar whose friendship I still treasure.

Sadly, my sister, Margret Reykdal, passed away in April 2019. My brothers and I are so glad that we had decided to host a special ninetieth birthday party for her in 2017. Margret had suggested that, to make it even more fun, we celebrate her big day in Lundar. It was quite the reunion, bringing us together from our far-flung homes in Edmonton, Canmore, Winnipeg, and Toronto. Rather than hold the party on Margret's actual birthday, which was in wintry November, we rescheduled it for the middle of summer. And so, on a beautiful day in July, about two dozen friends, family members, former neighbours, and classmates gathered for lunch at the Pauline Johnson Library on Lundar's main street, a block from the village's only school. The meal was catered by the library's board members. The main course was a selection of delicious salads and sandwiches, but the best part was the birthday cake. We all stood around the table, raised glasses of champagne, and sang "Happy Birthday" to our beloved sister as she blew out the candles.

CHAPTER 3

FROM BURNS TO BMO

When I applied for the job at Burns Bros. and Denton in 1963, the company used a psychological screening test to determine whether applicants were suitable for the investment banking and brokerage business. As I recall, the test indicated that my desire to be in a sales position was in the top 1 per cent. However, as I was a newcomer and had no knowledge of the industry, I decided to start as an analyst in the research department so I'd have a better understanding of the investments I would be recommending to our clients. Roland Bertin was the head of research at that time, and he was interested in hiring an analyst for the mining sector. Over the course of the next year, I authored two research reports, one on Noranda Mines (thirty-seven pages) and the other on Alcan Aluminum (twenty-eight pages), both then giants of the Canadian mining industry, but later taken over by foreign rivals.

At that time, Burns Bros. and Denton assigned a mentor to each new employee; it was my good fortune to have Don Boxer as mine. A former navy lieutenant in the Second World War, he was always quick to tell a joke, and he loved to golf. More importantly, he was a hard worker, and often offered suggestions to help improve my work. Don was a great networker, and I learned from his example that even later in your career, it's important to keep up your contacts. In short, he was a great mentor, and he and I became close friends.

Don was the role model of the partnership culture that was key to Burns Bros.' success. Part of this culture was placing the best interests of our clients first, and keeping partners' interests ahead of our own personal priorities. Charles Burns, his nephew Latham, Peter Eby, and Tim Beatty were great leaders and I learned a lot from them. Along with Don Boxer, Latham and Peter also became close friends. I will always remember the advice given to me by Tim Beatty, who was the firm's president at the time I joined: Regardless of what position you are in, focus on being the very best in what you do. Do not be concerned about being promoted. The cream always rises to the top!

In 1964, a year after joining the firm, I was transferred from the research department to institutional equity sales. I was also offered a position in Montreal, along with Bill Rogan, to start a desk serving clients in Quebec. I really enjoyed the move. We subsequently opened institutional sales desks in Vancouver, Calgary, Winnipeg, Halifax, and London, UK. Our goal was to be the number-one institutional equity trader in the business.

The previous decade, the postwar years, had been a time of rapid growth in Montreal. The city saw a huge influx of people from rural Quebec, as well as immigrants from the United Kingdom and elsewhere. At the time, it was also still a major financial centre; many of the corporate headquarters had not yet moved to Toronto. In 1965, the Canadian and Montreal stock exchanges, as they were then, moved to a new building, which at the time was the tallest in Canada and one of the most modern in the world. It was an exciting time to be in Montreal, but I didn't know many people. To connect with others in the financial community, I joined a new club for businessmen (yes, only men at the time) called The Whiff of Grape. It opened a chapter in Toronto a few years later, and I'm still a member. The club organized dinners (yes, with fine wines), debates, and guest speakers such as politicians, Olympians, and CEOs. It was a great way to expand my network.

Dorchester Boulevard, later renamed René-Lévesque Boulevard, was emerging as the centre of a newly developed downtown area, with many historical buildings being demolished to make way for skyscrapers. Burns Bros.' offices were at 1 Place Ville Marie, a set of four large towers at the corner of Dorchester Boulevard and University Street (now Robert-Bourassa Boulevard), completed in 1962, two years before my arrival.

My first task was to understand the investment objectives of each of our clients, which included mutual fund companies, pension funds, philanthropic foundations, and investment management firms. I then had to recommend investments that would help them achieve those objectives. Each day, I reviewed reports published by our research analysts and selected suitable stocks for each client. Because I had spent my first year as a mining analyst, I was initially more comfortable recommending stocks in the mining sector. However, it was essential to broaden my understanding to other sectors such as financial services, oil and gas, retail, conglomerates, and so on. Part of that process was to take my institutional clients out to lunch or dinner, and communicate with my colleagues on the sales desk and our analysts in the research department in Toronto, all of which I much enjoyed. My work was rewarded in 1967, when I was promoted to head of institutional equity sales. The downside was that it meant moving back to Toronto just before Montreal hosted the Expo 67 fair.

Connecting with even more institutional clients gave me a real appreciation for the benefits of networking. Many of them introduced me to interesting people from a wide variety of backgrounds, including executives in companies in which they had invested. They also often introduced me to their friends if we happened to be eating at the same restaurant.

I was also fortunate to maintain many of the contacts I had made in Montreal. One standout case was Jacques Ménard, whom I had already approached to join our firm when he was in the second year of his MBA at Western University, and we were keen to recruit more graduates from Western's Ivey Business School. Peter Eby and I interviewed Jacques again in 1974, when he was working for another brokerage firm. Peter and I both thought that he would be a great addition to Burns Bros. He had already established solid relationships with business leaders, politicians, and a number of not-for-profit groups in Quebec. Sure enough, Jacques joined us and went on to become one of the senior executives of BMO Financial Group and its president in Quebec. As Jacques recalls: "I was pretty young at the time, had just turned twenty-six. At that age, my contacts with local senior business-people and politicians was quite limited. That changed pretty quickly in the ten years following and beyond."[9]

The move back to Toronto also did wonders for my social life. Three years after returning from Montreal, in 1970, I went on a sailing vacation with a group that included one of the institutional salesmen in our London office, Henri Eschauzier. We rented a yacht named *Quetzalcoatl* and sailed off the coast of St. Tropez in France. During our time aboard, Henri mentioned that he had dated a girl in Toronto. He said she was very attractive and fun to be with, and suggested that, since I lived in Toronto, maybe I should get in touch with her. I took Henri's advice and gave her a call soon after returning to Canada. We had dinner, began dating, and about nine months later, on Saturday, June 5, 1971, we were married.

In 1976, Burns Bros. and Denton merged with Fry Mills Spence. Burns Bros.' strengths were primarily in the equity area, while Fry Mills Spence was a leader in debt markets. The two were very complementary but coming up with a name for the combined firm turned out to be a challenge. We first suggested Burns Bros. and Denton Fry Mills Spence. However, that seemed rather cumbersome, so both sides decided it made the most sense to choose one name from each of the two firms. The first name we came up with was Fry Burns—for obvious reasons, I suggested we should join the two predecessor names alphabetically as Burns Fry. Jack Lawrence, Fry Mills Spence's chief executive, became president of the combined firm, and Latham Burns, who had been president of Burns Bros., was named chairman.

One of my early moves after the merger was to persuade Barry Cooper, an institutional equity salesman who managed the Fry Mills Spence office in Montreal, to take charge of the combined institutional equity trading desk in Toronto. Barry was delighted to make the move; he viewed it as an opportunity to broaden his horizons beyond Quebec, and he was confident that it would advance his career. We became good friends, and remain so to this day. As Barry recalls:

> *Don Johnson was my boss when Burns Fry happened in 1976, and I was reporting to him. I liked Don from the get-go; he was a terrific leader. He was just the sort of person I enjoyed working with. He had the ability to be there if you*

needed him, not be all over you all the time, and to instill confidence. Don was always an incredibly positive person.[10]

Barry has reminded me that my office colleagues called me DK rather than Don at that time, and many still do. Although *D* and *K* are the initials of my first and middle names, the nickname actually stood for "Don't Know." Back in the 1970s, we had to balance our trades every morning. There were no computers in those days, so we would have to match the trades in our office with the trades recorded by the stock exchange. Inevitably, with so many trades happening every day, there would often be a "DK," meaning that traders had no idea how many shares they had bought or sold. We would have to figure out the discrepancies, which we nearly always did. "DK" became shorthand for problems in the office, and somehow, I got stuck with it.

Another nickname my colleagues gave me was Boggles. That was for the thick, Coke-bottle glasses I wore in those days, because of my poor eyesight. It would have been easy to take offence, but I never did. As Barry puts it: "If they stopped abusing you, you knew you were in trouble. The nicknames were all terms of endearment. We worked in a special environment."[11]

Around 1980, I took on responsibility for our research department and our retail brokerage division in addition to global institutional equity sales. Our goal was to be Canada's number-one-ranked research department in the annual Brendan Wood rankings, which were closely watched by industry analysts, as well as by our clients. I'm pleased to say that we achieved that goal several times. In particular, Hugh Brown, our highly regarded bank analyst, was ranked number one in his field for many consecutive years.

Don Johnson's father, Paul Bjorn Johnson (born Páll Björnsson), in front of his red barn with his racehorse "Prince," ca. 1930.

Don Johnson with friends John Christodoulou (centre) and Don Boxer (right), Majorca Island, late 1960s.

Don Johnson's mother, Fjóla Johnson, in Lundar, Manitoba, 1978.

A gathering at the family home in Lundar, Manitoba, with Don Johnson's brother, Paul Johnson (far left); Paul's wife, Ollie (kneeling in front); and Don's sister, Margret Reykdal (far right), 1984.

Don's friend David Appel, who is a member of goeasy's board, with his son James and wife, Carol, Toronto, 1987.

Pauline Johnson on her 100th birthday in Lundar, Manitoba, 1995.

Don Johnson with his three children in Zermatt, Switzerland, 1992.

Don's friends Nancy Holland and retired Ontario Supreme Court Judge Richard Holland in the south of France, 1993. Don and Anna bought their Caledon farm from the Hollands in 1989.

Don Johnson with Warren Buffett in Omaha, Nebraska, at the
Berkshire Hathaway offices, 1994.

Don Johnson outside the Pauline Johnson Library,
so named after Don Johnson and his siblings donated money
for a new library in Lundar, Manitoba, to
honour their former teacher on her 100th birthday.
The library was opened in 1998.

Hon. Roy MacLaren, Canada's High Commissioner to the United Kingdom, London, UK, 1998. Don had the opportunity to connect with Mr. MacLaren regularly during his many trips to London in the late 1990s, during work on the Imasco transaction.

Don and Anna Johnson's farm in Caledon, Ontario, 2000.

Don Johnson visiting Iceland with his family in 2005: brother Cy Johnson (fourth from left) and his wife, Carolann (far left); brother Paul Johnson (second from right) and, wife, Ollie (third from right).

Don Johnson with John Christodoulou at Don's home in Toronto, 2005.

Former Burns Fry colleagues (left to right):
John MacNaughton, Don Johnson, Barry Cooper,
and Hans Jurgen Queisser, Toronto, 2007.

Don Johnson with colleagues Don Boxer (centre) and Peter Eby
(right) at the Rosedale Golf Club, Toronto, 2009.

Unfortunately, my relentless focus on Burns Fry's success had begun to take a toll on my marriage. My first wife and I had three children, but the uncompromising nature of my work meant that I didn't have much flexibility to spend time with my children. Their mother concluded that I was not going to change my workaholic behaviour, and so, at her request, we separated in 1980.

In 1984 I was promoted to president of Burns Fry, and Jack Lawrence took over as chairman and CEO. I reported to Jack for five years until 1989, and this was a very difficult period for me. Certainly Jack was a highly successful business leader: under his stewardship, Burns Fry grew from a $10-million firm in the mid-1970s to its huge size and success in 1994, when it was purchased for $403 million by Bank of Montreal. But his business acumen was more than offset by his abrasive personality. To be blunt, I disliked Jack, and I don't think I was alone on the management team in feeling that way. He was a tough taskmaster, combative, and uninspiring. If there was one thing I learned from him, it was how *not* to manage people. Of the eight or nine executive committee members who worked under him when he was chairman, only two of us attended his funeral in 2009. The only reason I went to the memorial service was to reconnect with my former colleagues, but few of them were there.

■ ■ ■

By 1988, my partners at Burns Fry and I mutually agreed it was time for me to step down as president, and that my good friend and great partner John MacNaughton should succeed me. However, I was chairman of the Investment Dealers Association of Canada from 1988 to 1989, and we agreed I would remain president until I had completed my term.

This changing of the guard came to be overshadowed by momentous changes that swept through the entire Canadian securities industry in the late 1980s. Burns Fry was not immune to both the excitement and the anxiety that accompanied the turmoil, and by the time John took over as president, a new—and very different—era had dawned for the firm.

Prior to 1987, no one other than employees or partners was allowed to own more than 10 per cent of a Canadian investment dealer. What's more, Canada's financial services industry was split among four distinct "pillars": chartered banks, life insurance companies, trust companies, and investment dealers. But that changed in a dramatic way after the UK government, under Margaret Thatcher, launched an avalanche of deregulation, known as the Big Bang, which lifted many similar restrictions on players in the City of London.

Canada had little choice but to follow suit with a Little Bang. First Ontario and then the federal government responded with their own moves toward deregulation. In June 1987, the long-standing federal ownership rules were swept away, opening our securities industry to foreign players as well as to the big six domestic banks. The federal government said it would allow institutions to hold subsidiaries in other financial sectors, so, for example, banks would be allowed to sell insurance policies for the first time. The result was the arrival of a host of new players, notably the giant US investment banks and securities firms, and a spate of takeovers that targeted the Bay Street investment dealers.

Not surprisingly, Burns Fry was a prime target. We were a big player on Bay Street in the 1980s, and the Canadian banks were looking to buy up investment houses. Some of our competitors were keen to be acquired because it would give them access to the banks' vast financial resources.

Monte Kwinter, then Ontario's Minister of Financial Institutions and Minister of Consumer and Commercial Relations, trumpeted the changes with a prediction that by the time the dust from the Little Bang had settled, the industry would comprise some very strong Canadian players, some strong international players, and some niche players, But, he also warned, some would fall by the wayside.

That prediction mirrored my own feelings and those of my fellow partners at Burns Fry. We realized that deregulation was inevitable, and that it could vastly expand our horizons. We also recognized the benefits of having access to the big banks' balance sheets when competing with global banks for financing and merger and acquisition opportunities. On a more personal level, we were well aware of the hefty profit that we partners would likely reap from an acquisition of the firm. Even so, we had our doubts about the looming changes, especially the prospect of being swallowed by a big Canadian or foreign bank. We greatly enjoyed the Burns Fry partnership culture nurtured over many years: management and employees were shareholders and had the opportunity to make decisions after partners had reached a consensus. We were more than a little nervous that some of this camaraderie might be sacrificed if we were part of a much bigger organization.

It was clear from the outset of the Little Bang that the Canadian banks were itching to expand their footprint and acquire investment banking firms. There was a lot of speculation over which bank would climb into bed with which brokerage firm. Sure enough, over the course of 1987, Bank of Montreal acquired Nesbitt Thomson, and Bank of Nova Scotia bought McLeod Young Weir. RBC acquired Dominion Securities and CIBC snapped up Wood Gundy the following year. At Burns Fry, our top priority was to maintain a balance between having a new owner and preserving our partnership culture. To that end, we decided to engage a boutique advisory firm in the United Kingdom, Phoenix Securities, as our financial advisor. John Craven, who had extensive experience in the UK financial services business, founded his company to advise international securities firms on how to seize opportunities after the 1986 Big Bang. John connected us with a number of European investment banks as well as some US parties that were potentially interested in Burns Fry.

The partner that seemed to best fit our criteria was Security Pacific Merchant Bank, a division of Security Pacific Bank (SecPac), headquartered in Los Angeles. In 1987, it acquired 30 per cent of Burns Fry at three times book value. Peter Eby and Wil Matthews, one of our vice-chairmen, negotiated the deal from our side. The Americans said they wanted to have a call option on the remaining 70 per cent in the event they were not happy with the performance of Burns Fry's management. That would give them the right to immediately buy the remaining 70 per cent of Burns Fry's shares at the price originally agreed on, in other words, three times book value.

Peter agreed with this request, but we had much the same concern on our side. As Peter recalls, he told his SecPac counterpart: "If you have a call option at three times book value, we should have a put option in the event that we are not happy with the management of SecPac."[12] That gave us the right to have

SecPac purchase all the remaining Burns Fry shares immediately at the price agreed upon. SecPac quickly agreed, and we had a deal. It turned out to be a brilliant move by Peter.

Unfortunately, I missed out on much of the payout. Jack Lawrence had arbitrarily decided that some of the losses suffered by the firm after the Black Monday crash of 1987 were my fault. So, even though SecPac had agreed to pay three times the book value, Burns Fry bought back half of my shares in the firm at book value. That was maddening. I promptly ordered the personalized licence plate "1XBOOK."

Meanwhile, another romance was in the air. I had been dating Anna McCowan since 1981, and we were married on June 21, 1990, at Grace Church on-the-Hill in Forest Hill in Toronto. Latham Burns was my best man and his wife, Paddy Ann, was Anna's maid of honour. Anna had fourteen bridesmaids, and to match her, I had fourteen ushers and groomsmen. It was a match made in heaven and life was good to us. We were together for almost forty years until Anna's untimely death, the result of a fall, in August 2020.

I stepped down as president of Burns Fry in 1989, as arranged, and John MacNaughton succeeded me. SecPac offered me the position of chief executive of Security Pacific Alliance, a holding company for several investment banking and brokerage firms that it had acquired around the world. These included Hoare Govett in London, Hoare Govett Asia in Hong Kong, and McIntosh Hampson Hoare Govett in Australia. While SecPac was headquartered in LA, it made more sense for me to have an office in Toronto, because it was halfway between London and California. I simply kept the same office that I had at Burns Fry.

The relationship with Security Pacific did not go quite the way either side had planned. While the bank enjoyed an excellent AA+ credit rating when it acquired Burns Fry, by the early 1990s it was facing financial strain because of its heavy portfolio of sour real estate loans in Britain, Australia, and Arizona. The weak California real estate market had hit it hard too. BankAmerica (now Bank of America) bailed it out in 1991. However, because the Glass-Steagall Act was still in place in the United States, American banks were not permitted to own domestic investment banks. As a result, the new owners had little choice but to divest SecPac's investment banking and brokerage businesses. (SecPac had gotten around Glass-Steagall by setting up a subsidiary, Security Pacific Merchant Bank, which owned investment banks and brokerage businesses outside the United States.)

By then, the typical market value of an investment bank was the same as its book value. The Burns Fry partners threatened to exercise our put option, and after a year in the courts, we got BankAmerica to abandon its call option. That enabled us to acquire the shares held by BankAmerica at book value after exercising the Peter Eby put option at three times book value. Unwinding the 1987 deal meant that I returned to Burns Fry as vice-chairman with a focus on investment banking. Again, there was no need to move offices.

My job as vice-chairman was essentially to seek out new corporate clients, both in Canada and internationally. The first step in that process was to identify companies to which Burns Fry had not assigned a relationship manager. Two that came to mind immediately were Four Seasons Hotels and Resorts, based in Toronto, and Sun Company in Philadelphia, the integrated oil and gas producer later known as Sunoco. I chose Sun in Philadelphia because it owned 55 per cent of Suncor, which was the leader in developing the Alberta oil sands, a great growth industry.

My motives for seeking out Four Seasons were rather different. First, I had known Isadore "Issy" Sharp, the founder and chairman, for many years. Second, I was well aware that if I was the relationship manager for Four Seasons, I would have to stay at their fabulous hotels whenever I travelled internationally, regardless of Burns Fry's travel policy. What a perk that would be!

In February 1994, I was invited to deliver the James C. Taylor Distinguished Lecture in Finance at the Ivey Business School at Western University, my alma mater. I titled the lecture: "Bank Ownership of Investment Dealers: Synergies, Conflicts, Regulation, and Impact on Capital Markets." My remarks focused on my concern that, if a bank acquired Burns Fry, we would lose the decentralized, entrepreneurial culture of an employee-owned company and, instead, become part of a large bureaucracy. I was also concerned that we investment bankers would lose the opportunity to earn significant bonuses as our reward for attracting and executing financial and M&A transactions. If we were a bank subsidiary, our compensation would no doubt be calculated on the same basis as thousands of bank employees, and based more on seniority than on performance. Also, all major decisions affecting us would be made by senior executives at the bank, not by the partners of Burns Fry.

I noted in my lecture that integrating the two distinctly different cultures would be a challenge. Investment dealers constantly feel a sense of urgency and thrive on the excitement of "doing deals." But banks are larger and more bureaucratic, and decisions are made much more slowly with a greater emphasis on risk management. Senior bank executives spend a lot of time on long-term planning and in committee meetings. It would not be easy for the securities arm's chief executive to manage this distinction. I made the point that success would be determined by the CEO's willingness and ability to navigate the integration of the two cultures.

Some of my colleagues viewed my remarks as a career-limiting move, especially when, five months later in July 1994, we were acquired by Bank of Montreal. The bank paid $403 million in cash and shares, or about two times book value, and immediately merged Burns Fry with Nesbitt Thomson, which it had acquired at the time of the Little Bang. The new unit was given the name BMO Nesbitt Burns.

Brian Steck, who had been president of Nesbitt Thomson (the youngest ever, taking the helm when just thirty-one), became president of BMO Nesbitt Burns, and I stayed on as a vice-chairman. But just a few months after the deal, in the fall of 1994, Brian, a focused and calm but also relentless leader—he had at one time been a prospect for the Pittsburgh Pirates baseball team—invited me up to his office for a chat. He told me there were a lot of duplicated positions in the merged company and noted that a number of senior executives were well into their sixties. He knew that I was turning sixty on June 18, 1995, and suggested that might be an appropriate date for me to announce my retirement. He wanted to ensure that I had a reasonable retirement package and suggested that I retain the services of a lawyer to negotiate the terms with BMO's legal counsel. I was very disappointed with his suggestion; I had no interest in retiring. However, I had to face the fact that he was the boss.

My days at BMO may have been numbered, but I continued to work at full throttle. A few months later, in the spring of 1995, we concluded the acclaimed $1.1-billion Suncor transaction that I describe in Chapter 1. The ink was barely dry on that deal when I received another call from Brian. This time his message was rather different from our previous meeting. As far as I know, he had not been aware until then that I had been working on the Suncor sale as well as several other sizable deals. "Great work, Don," he said, and then went on to tell me that he and his colleagues recognized that I could still contribute to the firm and our clients, and that it was perhaps a little premature for me to retire on my sixtieth birthday.

I was both surprised and delighted when Brian arranged a new office for me so I could continue as a vice-chairman of BMO Nesbitt Burns, on salary. I considered this a great reward for a job well done. My focus would still be on identifying investment banking opportunities with Canadian and international companies with an interest in Canada. My significant network of contacts would be invaluable in finding those opportunities.

As things turned out, Brian and BMO would not regret their change of heart.

CHAPTER 4

A BIG DEAL

———

The seeds for the biggest deal of my entire career were planted in October 1997, as I read an article on the front page of the *Financial Times* on a flight from Johannesburg to London. The FT was reporting that the UK's British American Tobacco Industries (BAT) planned to spin off the financial services and retail assets that it had acquired several years earlier in a bid to diversify from its mainstay tobacco business. Its chief executive, Martin Broughton, planned to return the company to its tobacco roots.

The significance of this announcement hit me immediately. I knew that BAT had a 42 per cent stake in a Canadian conglomerate, Imasco Limited, which in turn owned 100 per cent of Imperial Tobacco, Canada's biggest tobacco company; CT Financial Services, better known as Canada Trust; Shoppers Drug Mart; and some real estate assets. No sooner had I checked in at the Four Seasons on London's Park Lane than I drafted a letter to Martin Broughton. The hotel concierge printed the letter on my letterhead, I signed it, and she immediately couriered it to BAT's offices. Essentially, I congratulated Martin on his decision to turn BAT back into a pure play tobacco company. I told him that we were aware that BAT owned 42 per cent of Imasco and that, no doubt, his logical objective would be to exchange that stake for a 100 per cent stake of Imperial Tobacco on the most tax-effective and financially attractive terms. I concluded with a promise to give him a call that afternoon to discuss whether he might be interested in us handling any such deal.

To my surprise, Martin, a straight talker in that no-nonsense British way, took my call and said he had forwarded my letter to Roger Lomax, head of corporate finance at BAT, whose main responsibility was to negotiate large and complex mergers and acquisitions transactions. BAT's investment in Imasco was on Roger's file, and Martin suggested I should call him and arrange a meeting.

I met Roger that same afternoon. He had a calm and unruffled disposition, and I grew to appreciate his smooth and steady presence when things got tricky. We had an informative and enjoyable chat, and I offered to take the initiative to conduct some research on the most advantageous financial and tax process for BAT to end up with 100 per cent of Imperial Tobacco.

Roger shared his perspective of these events when contacted as part of the research for this book:

> We had already, through Stikeman Elliott [the Montreal-based law firm], identified structures whereby our effective stake in Imasco's non-tobacco businesses might be realized. Acquisition of 100 per cent of Imperial Tobacco was not an overriding objective of BAT. It was not practicable simply to swap our shareholding in Imasco for control of Imperial Tobacco for the very good reason that the Imasco board would not have agreed to it. Imasco's primary objective was not the resolution of BAT's issues, but to merge CT with one of the chartered banks in return for shares, thereby gaining a

dominant minority shareholding and the ability to appoint its chairman.

Since disposal of the CT shareholding in one way or another would be the key to attaining BAT's objective, I encouraged Mr. Johnson to keep BAT informed of the developing situation in the Canadian banking sector and the willingness and capacity of the potential acquirers to enter into a transaction. An optimal transaction structure would require the acquisition of CT for cash simultaneously with a cash bid by BAT of the whole of the quoted majority of Imasco.[13]

For me, that meeting was the beginning of a most-rewarding two-and-a-half-year relationship with Roger. He was a real gentleman, with a great sense of humour, and I much enjoyed our time together. He had an intimate knowledge of Imasco and knew both the chairman and the CEO very well. We also had many common interests.

BAT retained the services of Stikeman Elliott for legal advice and the consultancy EY (formerly Ernst & Young) for accounting and tax advice. Purdy Crawford, a senior partner at the law firm Osler, Hoskin & Harcourt, was the chairman of Imasco and its previous president. Fortunately, I knew Purdy reasonably well. Born a coal miner's son in Nova Scotia, he was a man of integrity—and passionate about education, donating a lot of money to school and university programs. He was the kind of man whose door was always open. He introduced me to Brian Levitt, who was president and CEO of Imasco, and a former Osler partner. We also assembled a team of investment bankers under the leadership of Geoff Belsher, one of the senior investment banking partners at BMO Nesbitt Burns and a mergers and acquisitions expert. We had many meetings with lawyers, accountants, and investment bankers for the next several months.

I wrote to Roger Lomax every couple of weeks, updating him on what we had learned regarding the restructuring of Imasco. All of this effort, by the way, was on spec. As an investment banker, it was part of my job to identify potential investment banking opportunities like this one. During the following year and a half, I visited London eighteen times, meeting Roger either in his office or over lunch or dinner, depending on his preference. I jogged every day for a few miles around Hyde Park. My time in London also gave me an opportunity to reconnect with a number of friends, including Sir John Craven at Phoenix Securities, who had provided us with great advice when we were considering Burns Fry's future in the late 1980s. Among many others, I was able to connect regularly with Roy MacLaren, Canada's high commissioner in London at the time, and Peter Stormonth Darling, former chairman of Mercury Asset Management.

After a series of meetings with our legal and tax advisors, and our BAT/Imasco investment banking team, we concluded that the most tax-efficient way for BAT to exchange its 42 per cent of Imasco for 100 per cent of Imperial Tobacco would be for BAT to take Imasco private, increase the cost base of the non-tobacco-based businesses to fair market value, and then sell the non-tobacco businesses. All could be done without triggering any capital gains tax. Taking Imasco private would cost BAT about $10 billion, but it could not borrow such a large amount without breaking its debt covenants. All of the restructured debt was being allocated to its core tobacco business due to its positive and stable cash flow.

So we then recommended that BAT arrange for the sale of Canada Trust, Shoppers Drug Mart, and the real estate assets, but that these sales would close only when BAT had taken Imasco private. In this way, BAT could borrow the money from a bank syndicate as a short-term bridge loan, and then discharge the loan almost immediately from the proceeds of the sale of Canada Trust, Shoppers Drug Mart, and the real estate. BAT wanted confirmation from the federal government that raising the cost base of these businesses to fair market value was legally permissible under Canadian tax law. The Department of Finance duly confirmed that it did not have a problem with this strategy.

Canada Trust was the key asset, so it was important for BAT to find a buyer. No foreign financial institutions seemed interested, which left one of the big five Canadian banks as the only logical buyer. The problem was that any attempt to shop Canada Trust was greatly complicated by merger discussions among the banks. RBC and BMO had unveiled a plan in early 1998 to get together, as had TD Bank and CIBC. Both these deals were, of course, subject to government approval. At first blush, that left Scotiabank as the logical candidate for a pitch to consider taking over Canada Trust. Scotiabank publicly opposed any mergers involving its rivals, which was not surprising considering that it had been left as the odd man out and would be in a weakened competitive position. On the other hand, it would have been strange, if not downright hypocritical, for Scotiabank to consider acquiring the country's biggest trust company when it was lobbying against bank mergers. The bottom line for us was that none of the five banks was interested in discussing the acquisition of Canada Trust, leaving us in wait-and-see mode for a few months.

BAT would not officially engage us as their financial advisor for the going-private transaction until it knew that a deal could be done to raise the funds that it needed to buy out the Imasco minority shareholders. The prospects of that happening brightened markedly on December 14, 1998, when Minister of Finance Paul Martin stopped the bank mergers in their tracks. The main reason he gave was that the two new giant institutions would dominate Canada's financial services industry, leaving consumers with fewer choices and less competition. As Martin put it, the deals "would lead to an unacceptable concentration of economic power in the hands of fewer, very large banks."[14]

Shortly after the announcement, BAT engaged BMO Nesbitt Burns and Goldman Sachs as joint financial advisors on the Imasco transaction. The person we worked most closely with on the Goldman Sachs team was Doug Guzman. A few years later, Doug left Goldman and joined RBC Capital Markets, where he has had a stellar career. He became a managing director and head of global investment banking and, as of mid-2019, was head of RBC Wealth Management & RBC Insurance.

Even though Canada Trust was a trust company and not a bank, the question arose whether the authorities would once again raise concerns about it being acquired by one of the big banks. The bank that showed the keenest interest was TD, and Charlie Baillie, the president and CEO, worked on the project with Bill Brock, TD's deputy chairman and a former MBA classmate of mine at the University of Western Ontario. One of TD's advantages was that it had the strongest balance sheet of the banks because it had recently raised over $1 billion by taking public TD Waterhouse, its online brokerage business. Charlie and Bill smoothed the way for a deal by obtaining prior clearance from the federal government before even contacting BAT.

Roger Lomax has a valuable perspective on the negotiations that took place before the deal could go through:

> *The requirement for comfort from the Minister of Finance arose from the tax legislation which permitted the cost base of the assets of an acquired company to be raised to the amount paid in cash to acquire the company. This was known colloquially as a "bump." We had, with the help of Stikeman Elliott, familiarized ourselves thoroughly with the workings of the bump by the time BMO contacted us in 1997. If the transactions were for cash, there was no particular difficulty in obtaining the benefit of the bump. The only problem that arose was the discovery in April 1999 that TD had an investment in Imasco's listed preference shares. The legislation provided that the benefit of the bump could not be claimed where the purchaser of an asset had been a shareholder of the vendor. This threatened to vitiate the entire transaction. TD immediately sold the holding, but this was of no assistance.*
>
> *When the issue was raised with the finance ministry by Osler Hoskin representing Imasco and Stikeman Elliott representing BAT, the ministry indicated that they might be prepared to propose a change to the legislation to facilitate the transaction and to give a written undertaking to do so. We were advised that if such an undertaking were forthcoming, it would be safe to go ahead. The government was exceptionally accommodating since they were anxious for the sale of Canada Trust to go ahead.*

The merger agreement suggests that various rulings from Revenue Canada and the Quebec revenue agency were required as conditions to closing. These would have been obtained by Stikeman. I don't recall being aware of or seeing any confirmation from the finance ministry obtained by BMO, although it is quite possible that they consulted the authorities in the course of preparing their proposal to BAT. [15]

Once TD was on board, Roger wasted no time flying over to Toronto. Word reached me that he and Bill Brock were having dinner at Scaramouche restaurant in Forest Hill to discuss the next steps, and I sent in a bottle of champagne as a gesture of appreciation. After extensive negotiations, the terms were agreed upon, with TD paying $7.85 billion for Canada Trust. The transaction would close in early February 2000.

In parallel with this process, we also contacted prospective buyers of Shoppers Drug Mart. After protracted talks with a number of interested parties, the Ontario Teachers' Pension Plan and Kohlberg Kravis Roberts & Co. (KKR), the well-known New York buyout firm, agreed to acquire Shoppers jointly for about $2.6 billion, with the deal closing on the same day as the Canada Trust sale.

Meanwhile, Geoff Belsher assembled a large team of about ten investment bankers to help negotiate Imasco's going-private transaction, with support from legal and tax advisors. They played a key role in forging an agreement, working tirelessly for countless hours, seven days a week—and ordering in a good many pizzas.

The total cost for BAT to acquire the remaining 58 per cent of Imasco was about $10 billion, with the transaction set to close on February 1, 2000. Most of the funds came from the Canada Trust sale, but BAT also arranged a bridge loan to fund the deal. As Roger Lomax recalls:

> *The requirement for a bridge loan was some $2.5 billion, essentially to cover the period between closing of the main transaction and disposal of Shoppers Drug Mart. In the event, the sale of Shoppers to a consortium assembled by KKR was closed in the same week as the main Imasco transaction, so that the facility was drawn for only three days.*[16]

The outcome was a win-win for all concerned. BAT was able to achieve what Geoff Belsher colourfully described as its "buy, bump, and sell" strategy. BAT exchanged its 42 per cent stake in Imasco for 100 per cent of Imperial Tobacco without incurring any capital gains tax on the sale of Canada Trust or Shoppers Drug Mart, thereby achieving its goal of gaining total control of Imperial without any extra investment. As for Imasco's shareholders, they scored a premium of more than 25 per cent compared to the price of their shares prior to the start of media speculation about the deal. TD received a big boost by acquiring Canada Trust, with its sizable retail branch network across Canada. Ed Clark, Canada Trust's chief executive, went on to succeed Charlie Baillie at the helm of TD Bank Group.

BMO Nesbitt Burns benefited handsomely by generating tens of millions of dollars in advisory fees for the going-private transaction, the largest in the history of the bank and its predecessor companies. We also earned significant fees from related underwriting transactions, such as the TD Waterhouse IPO. I was rewarded with a bonus. To cap it all, Canada Trust, which had been controlled by a London-based conglomerate, was now under the wing of a Canadian bank, while Shoppers Drug Mart was in the hands of a Canadian pension plan (together with a US investment firm).

We had finally made it happen. It had been more than two years since I had seen the FT article that sparked the idea of contacting Martin Broughton at BAT. The deal was the most interesting, challenging, complex, and satisfying one in my investment banking career. Sometimes, the atmosphere had been like a pressure cooker. Twelve-hour workdays were often the norm, which clearly did not help my work-life balance. Besides running every morning to burn off some of the stress, I had taken up transcendental meditation in order to remain clear-headed throughout high-pressure period such as this. I have much more to say on TM in Chapter 8.

After all of the transactions had closed, we arranged a fabulous closing dinner—champagne and the whole works—in a private room at the Toronto Club, with members of the teams from Imasco, BAT, BMO Nesbitt Burns, Goldman Sachs, Stikeman Elliott, and Ernst & Young. It was a great celebration, fully justified given the hard work we had all done.

That evening, I couldn't help but reflect how far the firm and my own career had come since my start with Burns Bros. and Denton as a research analyst way back in 1963. Of course, not all transactions worked out as well as the Imasco one did. I have worked on a few that were far less successful but, as I'd soon discover, even bad deals sometimes have silver linings.

CHAPTER 5

A GREAT CANADIAN SUCCESS STORY

I have been chairman of goeasy and its predecessor companies, easyhome and RTO Enterprises, since 2000, when it had a market cap of less than $10 million, and became chairman emeritus in 2019. Now a successful leader in rent-to-own and non-prime lending, goeasy has more than 1,800 employees and, as of January 2020, a market value of over $1 billion.

My involvement began more than three decades ago on Black Monday, October 19, 1987. The market crash that day made it difficult to raise equity capital, which was probably why I received a call the next day from a broker, Murray Sinclair, telling me that only two companies in the world were still making plans to go public. One was British Petroleum, the multinational energy giant, and the other was a small Canadian outfit called Rentown—a play on the words rent-to-own—which was in the business of leasing home electronics, furniture, and appliances to consumers until they paid enough—including a big chunk of interest—to gain ownership of the asset.

Murray and I competed in the investment banking and brokerage business, and we called each other regularly to chat about the market and share ideas. I told Murray that while I was obviously familiar with BP, I had never heard of Rentown. He explained that the two leading rent-to-own companies in the United States were Rent-A-Center and Aaron's, and that Rentown was becoming a force to be reckoned with in Canada.

Rentown's head office was in Edmonton, and it turned out that its founder, president, and chief executive was none other than my nephew Gordon Reykdal, son of my older sister Margret.

I knew that Gordon had a reputation as an astute salesman. He was a great promoter and could be very convincing when he wanted to be. He was also young—just thirty in 1987—charismatic, and very confident about the future of his businesses.

Murray was looking for investors in Rentown's IPO, and I was glad to support it, not only because Gord was my nephew but also because Rentown had a high-growth outlook and fragmented competition. I initially invested $100,000. It seemed like the kind of little-known but promising opportunity that investment bankers are always looking for.

Rentown grew rapidly after the IPO through a two-pronged strategy of opening new stores and acquiring existing outlets from its rivals. Gordon also negotiated a $25.3 million demand loan in August 1988 from Transamerica Commercial Finance Corp., a US financial services company, to help finance acquisitions and pay back the private investors. All of Rentown's assets were pledged to Transamerica, and Gordon personally guaranteed the loan.

Fast-forward to November 1989. I was still president of Burns Fry when Gord contacted me to ask if we could raise some equity capital to finance Rentown's growth plans. Again, because he was my nephew and the company appeared to be doing well, I was glad to support him. My colleagues did some due diligence on the company, and we ended up leading a $5-million equity financing in January 1990: I placed a personal "lead order" for

$1 million, and a significant portion of the balance was placed with friends of mine who were also clients of the firm. I was confident that the stock had considerable upside potential.

Alas, my optimism turned out to be misplaced. Less than a year later, in November 1990, we were at a dinner at Centro restaurant in Toronto to celebrate closing the deal. As dessert was being served, we heard that Transamerica was calling in its loan because Rentown was losing money and not meeting the conditions of its loan facility. The company went bankrupt soon after, in late January 1991.

From looking like a sure-fire winner, Rentown had turned into the most embarrassing transaction in my entire investment banking career. I called each of the friends who had put money into the equity financing and expressed my sincere apologies for recommending the company. Understandably, they were not too happy, though most took some comfort from the fact that I had put my own money where my mouth was with a significant personal investment. It was a costly mistake for all of us, and ended with Transamerica taking over all of Rentown's fifty stores across Canada.

Undaunted, Gord incorporated another rent-to-own business, RTO Enterprises, in December 1990, and took it public two-and-a-half years later through a reverse takeover of a public company. Perhaps because of the family connection, I naively assumed that he had learned from his previous mistakes. I helped RTO negotiate the purchase of the fifty Rentown stores from Transamerica, plus a bank facility to finance the deal. RTO was able to buy the Rentown stores from Transamerica for $10.8 million, which was just one-third of Transamerica's earlier loan to Rentown. The bank loan was repaid within eighteen months.

Gordon found private investors willing to put money into each new store, and once that outlet was cash positive, he would pay back the investment, with a suitable profit. Again, I became an investor in Gord's company, ending up as RTO's largest individual shareholder.

Gord hired a chief operating officer, Mac Hennigan, from another US rent-to-own company called Magic Rentals, which happened to be a subsidiary of Transamerica. Mac was in charge of RTO's day-to-day operations. He was a good man, but unfortunately, he took ill and had to step down abruptly. A year went by and Gord had still not hired a new COO, partly because there were no suitable candidates in Canada, given that RTO was the only significant rent-to-own company north of the border. It was increasingly apparent that the only credible successor to Mac would be a seasoned executive from either Rent-A-Center or Aaron's in the United States who was willing to move north.

Our opportunity came in 1998, when Thorn Americas, the US subsidiary of a well-known British electrical engineering and rentals company, sold Rent-A-Center, which had about 1,400 stores, to another US player, Renter's Choice, for US$900 million. The debt was supplied by asset management firm Apollo. As with most other leveraged buyouts, Renter's Choice needed to find big savings to service the debt and make the deal a success. That meant merging the two companies' head offices, and squeezing local governments for the biggest possible tax concessions. To that end, Renter's Choice chair and CEO, Ernie Talley, relocated the company from Wichita, Kansas, to his hometown of Plano, Texas. But only 6 of Rent-A-Center's 550 employees in Wichita made the move. That left a lot of seasoned rent-to-own executives looking for jobs and gave RTO the perfect opening to attract a new chief operating officer from Wichita to Edmonton.

I asked two former chief executives of Thorn Americas and one former head of the parent group in London for suggestions of potential candidates. All three recommended David Ingram, a young Englishman whom Thorn had moved across the pond to learn the rent-to-own business at Rent-A-Center. Though David was only thirty-two years old, he was already the divisional vice-president for 380 US stores, and had overseen 29 stores in Canada before they were sold to RTO Enterprises in 1997. Next, I contacted Bud Gates, a former Rent-A-Center CEO who lived in Wichita, and asked if he would line up any other former Rent-A-Center executives who might be suitable for the number-two job at RTO. I ended up flying down to Kansas and interviewing about half a dozen candidates, including David Ingram. I short-listed three, but David was my top pick. At that time, he was also being interviewed for a top position at Thorn Asia, based in Sydney, Australia, as well as for the job of divisional manager for three hundred Woolworths stores in the UK.

I then called Gord Reykdal in Edmonton with the suggestion that he go down to Wichita to interview the three shortlisted RTO candidates. I conveyed my view to him that David Ingram was clearly the best choice. What's more, David was still single at the time and would be happy to move to Alberta. Gord duly met the three candidates, but much to my surprise, his pick was one of the others: a man named Paul Barry, who lived in Chicago and was unwilling to move to Canada. Gord was the CEO, so we had little option but to go along with his choice. Paul Barry became number two at RTO, and David Ingram moved back to the UK, where he took up the senior position at Woolworths.

I had no doubt that Gord had made a big mistake. David was clearly head and shoulders above the other candidates, and I was very frustrated.

Besides the contrast in the two men's management skills, it made no sense at all for a Canadian company to have its chief executive and head office in Edmonton, but its chief operating officer sitting in Chicago. I joined the board of directors in 1999, as I became increasingly concerned about the company's management as well as its financial condition and accounting practices.

Not surprisingly, RTO's financial performance continued to deteriorate, to the point that by the spring of 2000, it was teetering on the brink of insolvency. The shares tumbled from a high of $5.45 in 1996 to around $1 four years later. The company reported a net loss of $1.1 million in the final quarter of 1999, by which time Gord was talking about taking it private.

This situation presented not only a business challenge but also a personal dilemma for me. Gord may have been my nephew, but a number of my close friends had signed on as shareholders in Rentown, and subsequently in RTO. As I recall, I did not approach any friends to invest the second time around, but perhaps when they heard that I was willing to put up some money, they decided to come in too. As the largest shareholder, with more than 14 per cent of the shares as of May 2000, I believed I had a moral obligation to save RTO. And the most obvious way to do that was to shake up its senior management.

I obtained solid legal advice from my then friend Wes Voorheis. Wes's recommendation was that I meet with Gord and tell him that if he did not step aside as chair and CEO, I would launch a proxy fight prior to the annual meeting at the end of June 2000 and propose my own slate of directors. The plan was to shift Gord into the vice-chair position where he would have little executive authority. Between my equity stake and those of my friends, I was confident that a majority of shareholders would back me.

There was one big hurdle in my way, however. At that time, apart from David Lewis, whom I had known since the 1960s when he was my personal banker at CIBC, all the members of RTO's board were Gord's allies. What's more, the directors had approved a very generous severance package for Gord in the event that he was ever terminated as CEO. The centrepiece of this sweetheart deal was a $1.375-million cash payment. As it turned out, Gord had already received about $300,000 of this amount, as RTO was hurtling toward bankruptcy, and the company could not afford to pay him the remaining $1 million. Because he was my nephew, I lent RTO that amount to cover the balance of his severance package. He duly agreed to become vice-chair, but quit a month later to start up a payday loan company.

That was the last of any business dealings I would have with my nephew. Gord went on to expand a payday loan company, Rentcash (later Cash Store Financial Services), through a series of acquisitions and new store openings. It went public at about $1 per share, and within a few years the shares were trading at close to $30. Indeed, Cash Store grew to be the second-largest payday loan operator in Canada, with several hundred stores. But twelve years after it went public, it too went bankrupt, in 2014. Nor was that the end of Gord's troubles. In a final humiliation, he agreed to a settlement with the Alberta Securities Commission in September 2020 in which he admitted authorizing misrepresentations in the Cash Store's financial statements. As part of the deal, he agreed to pay $300,000 to the commission, plus $200,000 in costs, and was barred from serving as an officer or director of any public company for two years. He also agreed to attend training "in best practices for public company governance and disclosure."

As my experience with Gord proved, having a family member as a business partner is never easy. It can be tough to separate family loyalties from the emotionally detached decisions so often required to run a successful business. I'm pleased to say, however, that although my relationship with Gord was a turbulent one, it did not sully ties with my sister Margret and her other children, Diane, Bruce, Greg, and Steve. I was close to my sister until her passing in April 2019 and remain close with my other nephews and niece to this day.

After taking the chair at RTO and reviewing the financial statements, I discovered that the company was not only insolvent but also that its books were a mess, with many irregularities. We retained Ernst & Young to audit the company, and it found that far from the reported net income of $197,276 for the first quarter of 2000, RTO had in fact racked up a loss of $93,494. We urgently needed a board with expertise in four different areas—finance, accounting, the rent-to-own business, and Canadian retailing. I was able to fill these gaps with five worthy new directors: Robin Korthals, former president of TD Bank; Ron Gage, former chairman and CEO of Ernst & Young Canada; Doug Anderson, former CEO of Rent-A-Center in the US; Joe Rotunda, former COO of Rent-A-Center; and Bruce Reid, former chief executive of The Brick Warehouse. We asked Bruce to take the reins as interim CEO. The only two directors who remained from the previous board were David Lewis and Gerald McCarvill, president of financial services firm McCarvill Corporation.

Meanwhile, I had stayed in touch with David Ingram, my top pick for the number-two job back in 1998. My dream was to convince him to move back to North America, this time to Canada, and to take the top spot at RTO. I wasted no time once the new board was in place. In June 2000, I arranged for David to fly from London to Toronto for a weekend. I introduced him to Robin Korthals, Ron Gage, and Bruce Reid, and arranged for him to visit some stores incognito. We quickly agreed that David was our man and made him an offer. But his bosses at Woolworths moved heaven and earth to persuade him to stay in the UK. I eventually prevailed, but not without going above and beyond. We agreed on terms shortly before David married his American fiancée Jennifer on the Isle of Wight. But knowing the pressure he was feeling from Woolworths, I was still nervous that he might back out, so I decided to try and track him down on his honeymoon in the Maldives. My assistant finally managed to contact Jennifer's parents, who thankfully had the phone number of the resort where they were staying. David and I had a good discussion from opposite ends of the world about the possibility of him taking the job. Fortunately, Jennifer also liked the idea, not least because she was originally from Kansas, and Toronto is a lot closer than London to Kansas. The couple had met in 1997, when they were both employees of Thorn Group, which owned Rent-A-Center. To my delight, David subsequently called me from the Maldives to confirm that he would be joining us. He had to give proper notice to Woolworths, so we agreed that he would join RTO in December 2000 as executive vice-president and chief operating officer, and formally succeed Bruce Reid as CEO at some point in the future.

Besides installing fresh management, our top priority was to address the company's financial crisis, and that meant raising at least $5 million in new equity. Because several friends had been long-suffering and loyal RTO shareholders, I wanted to give them an opportunity to participate in the financing if they were willing to take yet another gamble on the rent-to-own business. We announced a rights issue in the fall of 2000, but the Ontario Securities Commission refused to approve the financing on the grounds that the company would be bankrupt if the issue was not fully subscribed. I once again decided to step into the breach, with a promise to buy any leftover shares. As it turned out, almost half of the rights issue was not subscribed, which meant that I had to put up about $2.6 million, making me RTO's biggest shareholder, with over 30 per cent of the equity. This time, my investment in the rent-to-own business turned out to be one of the smartest I ever made.

RTO lost $9 million in 2000, but the new management team was determined to turn a profit the following year. The company had no spare cash and all suppliers were demanding cash on delivery, so there were no credit terms for payments. Management reviewed every cost item and negotiated capital at a lower cost. These efforts were rewarded with a $1 million profit in 2001.

David Ingram then started testing various formats for refreshing and consolidating RTO's five brands. Focus groups came up with some one hundred possible new names for the company. David didn't like any of them, so he asked the market research agency to give him the two words that came up most often in the focus groups. The answer was that participants wanted transactions to be "easy," and the most important thing in their life was their "home." So, in July 2003, all 131 RTO locations were remodelled and renamed easyhome. Even the ticker symbol was changed to EH—how Canadian can you get? To cap the changes, in 2006 David hired Chris Fregren, a chartered accountant and former vice-president of finance at mutual fund group AGF Management, as vice-president and chief financial officer. Around that time, we also moved the head office from Edmonton to Mississauga. It made sense on all counts. Bill Johnson, the outgoing CFO, was the last remaining executive working from Alberta. On the other hand, David lived in Toronto and needed to build his management team there.

David had begun considering new growth areas in 2005 since he believed that the leasing business in Canada was nearing saturation point. He also had the wisdom to realize that the best time for a business to test new ventures was when it was enjoying strong growth with excess capital to invest. A handful of concepts were agreed upon and models were built to ensure that they stayed within a budgeted investment range, so that failure would not have a material impact on current cash flow or profitability. If any of these initiatives showed promise, then we would step up the financial commitment.

One such idea came to David in October 2005, when he was in Edmonton, completing his monthly financial reviews with the accounting team. While having a drink in the hotel bar, he drew a graph on a napkin: one axis showed interest rates from low to high, and the other the level of risk. The illustration led David to conclude that a significant gap existed in the market between the low rates charged on ultra-safe, secured bank loans and the 500 per cent annual interest charged by payday loan companies. The key insight was that the average payday loan customer was taking out three loans from different lenders for a total debt of $1,500, but could never hope to repay the full balance every pay cycle. David saw a potentially lucrative opening for a lender limiting its interest rate to the federal criminal code cap of 60 per cent a year, while holding loss rates below 20 per cent. And so a new business, easyfinancial, was born.

The first easyfinancial kiosk opened three months later on January 19, 2006, inside easyhome's first leasing store, on Stony Plain Road in Edmonton. Like easyhome, easyfinancial catered to cash- and credit-constrained consumers. The kiosks were initially built inside easyhome locations as a low-cost way to test the concept and to monitor demand and performance. We began by offering instalment loans of $1,500 to $3,000 amortized over twelve months so that approved payday loan customers could consolidate their loans, thereby reducing their interest expense by up to 90 per cent as well as giving themselves extra time to repay the loans. The loan book was financed by free cash flow from the leasing business, with no external funding required. We carefully controlled the growth of kiosks to ensure that the company's consolidated profit continued to grow at a compound rate of more than 20 per cent.

Then came the 2007–08 financial crisis. In one sense, the upheavals in the US financial services industry created a huge business opportunity for easyhome and easyfinancial, but it also sowed the seeds for a big battle within the board of directors that would rage for several years to come.

As politicians debated the causes of the subprime mortgage collapse and studied the carnage of the banks destroyed in its wake, committees were formed to introduce new rules and oversight. To that end, in December 2009, the Basel Committee on Banking Supervision proposed a set of capital and liquidity standards for the global banking sector. The reforms, known as Basel III, were passed by the Group of Twenty (G20) leading economies in November 2010, and the committee left it to each member state to implement the standards individually. The US response took the form of the Wall Street Reform and Consumer Protection Act, commonly known as the Dodd-Frank Act, which was passed by the US Congress in 2010 and required banks with more than US$50 million in assets to abide by more stringent capital and liquidity standards. The new law meant that banks had to set aside more capital for riskier loans, thus reducing the profitability of non-prime lending. What's more, those involved in this type of lending had increasingly found themselves in the crosshairs of public and media criticism. Many decided to take the path of least resistance and simply get out of the sub-prime business. But, as they say, one man's problem is another's opportunity, and it gradually became clear that the US banks' discomfort was creating a lucrative opening for easyhome and easyfinancial.

Of special interest to us were the three banks that dominated subprime lending in Canada: Wells Fargo, HSBC Finance, and CitiFinancial. These three operated about one thousand non-prime lending branches across Canada, and held a combined loan book of about $12 billion in secured and unsecured loans and mortgages. Wells Fargo and HSBC ran off their loan books and closed their branches. CitiFinancial focused on its balance sheet and shrank its loan book before selling the operation to US equity funds in 2017, which rebranded the business as Fairstone. The bottom line was that with the big US players retreating from the non-prime business, there was an enormous opportunity to service over a million Canadian customers who still had an appetite for consumer loans. Seeing the gap, easyhome wasted no time filling it.

But amidst the excitement and the growth trajectory that we were plotting came the biggest threat that the company had experienced since David took charge in May 2001. In 2010, easyfinancial hired Jason Mullins, a smart and ambitious young man, to run its online lending operation. The first big task that David assigned to Jason was to conduct a forensic audit on easyfinancial's branch in Saint John, New Brunswick, seemingly its most successful location. Although the branch had passed all the normal audit checks, its stellar performance also left a sense of unease in the top management team. Much digital analysis and the discovery of false social insurance numbers on customer accounts led Jason to the conclusion that the local manager was creating fake loans, essentially running a Ponzi scheme. The manager was fired immediately, but we were forced to take a hefty one-time charge of $3.4 million.

The saga was a huge punch in the gut for all of us, but as so often happens when adversity strikes, it taught us one of the most valuable lessons in our history: the need to strengthen our risk-management procedures and governance. All lending moved from local adjudication to central decision-making, and cash payments were replaced by electronic direct debits to minimize the risk of fraud. More generally, the Saint John fraud was a wake-up call for a management team that up till then had known only success, but now had to adjust to board and shareholder scrutiny. But there was a silver lining, too. Impressed by how Jason Mullins had handled the investigation and its aftermath, David saw an opening for succession planning and promoted Jason to head easyfinancial.

Meanwhile, we needed to start recruiting new directors to replace several who were about to retire. The first of the new cohort was Wes Voorheis, the lawyer who had given me such valuable advice prior to the RTO Enterprises annual meeting in 2000. Four more seats on the board opened up in 2009 and 2010. One of the replacements was my friend David Appel; another was Jamie Bowland, a former partner at Burns Fry who approached me after his retirement from BMO Capital Markets a short time earlier. Wes put forward the names of two friends, Steve Richardson and Rod Adams, and they were also brought on board.

Sadly, my relationship with Wes after he joined the board in 2010 turned out to be quite a contrast to his helpfulness ten years earlier. Unbeknownst to me, he had often acted as a stalking horse for shareholder activists, joining boards of directors on behalf of dissident shareholders who believed that the management and board of a public company were either incompetent or untrustworthy. Wes wasn't afraid of a fight. I think he honestly believed that he was doing what was right for shareholders, but in easyhome's case, I completely disagreed.

As the easyfinancial unit continued to grow, Wes became increasingly vocal in questioning what he saw as the high risks of subprime lending. The fraud at the Saint John kiosk was a major concern, and he thought we faced similar risks in other parts of the country. He called frequent board and committee meetings to discuss whether we should remain in this business. For my part, I was 100 per cent behind David Ingram and Jason Mullins in expanding the subprime business, and I had a high level of confidence in their ability to address the risks. In any case, I took the view that key operational decisions should be left to management, not made by the board of directors. Wes vehemently disagreed, and the board became increasingly polarized.

The disagreements came to a head at 5 p.m. on Friday, December 9, 2011, when Wes and Jamie Bowland showed up unannounced at my office with an ultimatum. Wes sat down in a chair facing my desk and calmly drew my attention to a provision in easyhome's bylaws under which any two directors could call a special board meeting on forty-eight hours' notice. He told me that he was proposing to do just that, with the meeting scheduled for 9 a.m. the following Monday. He planned to table a resolution that the board replace me as easyhome's chair with one of his allies. He was direct and calm, though clearly there was no room for negotiation or compromise. It was immediately clear to me that the real purpose of the coup was to remove David Ingram as chief executive and replace him with another of Wes's pals on the board. But Wes was well aware that the only way to get rid of David was to remove me as chair. His parting shot that afternoon was to tell me that he and Jamie had already secured the support of five of the nine directors. They would see me at Wes's office at 9 a.m. on Monday.

I later learned that Wes was also incensed by my acquisition around that time of another 900,000 shares in easyhome, taking my ownership to over 27 per cent of the total. A friend later told me that this was a catalyst for the ensuing fight, though I'm puzzled to this day why that would have upset Wes.

I was totally shocked by the confrontation and knew I needed legal advice in a hurry so that I could consider my options over the weekend. I immediately contacted Rob Staley at Bennett Jones and arranged to meet him early Saturday morning. Rob knew Wes and had acted for him, and opposite him, in a number of lawsuits. I also asked a friend at Torys LLP to put me in touch with a corporate governance expert. He introduced me to Jamie

Scarlett, and we met on Saturday afternoon. To ensure that we were all on the same page, the three of us spoke together by phone on the Sunday afternoon.

Monday morning came, and all the board members convened in Wes Voorheis's office. Wes outlined the purpose of the meeting, and each director was given an opportunity to speak his mind (yes, it was still an all-male board at that time) about his concerns. It soon became clear that the five dissidents were sticking to a collective script on why I should step aside as chair. But David Appel and David Lewis vigorously defended management and me, telling the others that their sudden attempt at a coup was unjustified and unacceptable. I then made the following statement:

> *Wes, before you put your resolution to a vote, you and your four board members should consider the following facts. Four of you don't own a single share in easyhome, and one of you owns five thousand shares. I, as chair, own more than three million shares. If you put this resolution to a vote you may wish to consider the possibility that I might call a special shareholders meeting and put forth my own slate of directors. You can imagine who would not be on the list!*

The five directors left the meeting and returned shortly to say that the meeting would be adjourned, and we would reconvene on Wednesday morning at 9 a.m.

Then began a flurry of activity behind the scenes. David Ingram reached out to Jamie Bowland to see if they could find a pragmatic solution to the dissidents' insistence that I be removed as chairman. David's proposal was that I would become vice-chair and Jamie would move into the chairman's role. The plan was designed to keep the dissidents in check while, at the same time, ensuring that if they continued to rock the boat, then we could use my ownership position to outflank them. However, Wes—ever the skeptic—saw a problem. He insisted that he and his allies would agree to the change only if I committed to voting all my shares in line with the board's wishes for the next two years. Essentially, this tactic would mean that they could call all the shots even though they owned only 5,000 shares among them.

Wednesday morning arrived and I immediately informed the board that I would definitely not agree to voting all of my shares in line with the board's wishes for the next two years.

Wes responded by asking for a private session with his four allies before proceeding further. When they came back thirty minutes later, he dropped a bombshell: not only would he and Jamie resign but so too would the other dissidents. Clearly, hard facts and good sense had won the day.

All in all, I'm glad how things turned out. Had any of the dissident directors decided to stay, we would still have been burdened by a dysfunctional board, which would have made it much tougher to manage the company in the years to come. With all five out of the way, we had a clean slate to bring in fresh blood that would add value and that I could trust. To this day, I bear Wes no ill will; he did us a big favour by arranging for all five directors to resign simultaneously, and for that I owe him a debt of gratitude.

While my remaining three colleagues and I were delighted with the dissidents' decision, the markets were initially unimpressed by news of a mass resignation of easyhome directors. The stock dropped from almost $7 to just above $5. But the sellers clearly did not fully grasp the circumstances surrounding the resignations, nor the potential of the company. Anyone who sold their shares in late 2011 would have learned an expensive lesson. From December 2000 until 2018, easyhome boasted the thirteenth-highest shareholder return of any company listed on the TSX. The engine driving the company's growth was (and still is) easyfinancial. By January 2020, goeasy was trading at about $70 a share, a stunning two hundred and fifty times more than an investor would have paid in 2001.

We now had only four directors: myself and the three Davids—Ingram, Appel, and Lewis. We did not need to replace all five dissidents immediately, but I thought we should add at least three new members to the board. The chief criterion for selection was that each of the newcomers would have to add some value and, ideally, be known to at least one of the existing directors. My pick was David Jon Thomson, a classmate from the MBA class of 1963 at Western. David had extensive experience in the real estate business with Oxford Development Group and Great-West Life. A Toronto resident, he had also sat on the boards of several public companies. For the second spot, we chose Sean Morrison from Vancouver. Sean was managing partner at Maxam Capital Corporation, which had a significant equity stake in easyhome. We were also keen to have at least one woman on the board; after all, half of our employees and half of our customers were female. Sean later introduced us to Karen Basian, whose extensive business experience included senior positions at McCain Foods and Frito-Lay North America. We may have lost five directors, but we had found three excellent replacements.

easyfinancial's loan book continued to grow exponentially, while the lease-to-own business under the easyhome label was basically stable, generating cash flow that helped finance that growth. The contrasting performance of the two brands presented a problem. The dominant business was becoming easyfinancial, but the parent company's name was easyhome—which represented the less glamorous, slower-growing lease-to-own business. In September 2015, management decided to give the public company a zippy new name: goeasy. This parent company had two subsidiaries, easyfinancial and easyhome, sending a clear message to the market that we now had two core businesses.

Delighted as we were with easyfinancial's success, rapid growth also presented three important challenges: first, maintaining a strong management team to advance the company's growth strategy; second, financing that growth; and third, ensuring we contained the risks inherent in subprime lending.

David Ingram and Jason Mullins began to tackle these issues with a number of senior appointments: Andrea Fiederer as executive vice-president and chief marketing officer; Shane Pennell as senior vice-president for operations and shared services; Jason Appel as senior vice-president and chief risk officer; Shadi Khatib as senior vice-president and chief information officer; David Cooper as senior vice-president of human resources; and Steven Poole as senior vice-president of operations and merchandising.

Financing was a real challenge because the big Canadian banks do not typically lend to companies in the unsecured lending business. As David Yeilding, goeasy's chief financial officer, puts it: "I'm not aware of anyone apart from the original group of HSBC, Wells Fargo, or CitiFinancial ever getting bank support for unsecured non-prime lending."[17]

Instead, easyfinancial turned to the United States, starting in October 2012, with a syndicate of funds led by Crystal Financial that put up CA$20 million in loans. This grew over the next two years to $200 million, with the cost falling from about 10 per cent to 8.5 per cent as the company's financial performance improved. While the Crystal Financial loans gave easyfinancial the resources to expand significantly, we needed additional financing as the loan book continued to grow. For several years, Wells Fargo was one of our targets. Management met with the California-based bank in 2017, but could not negotiate a loan facility until BMO Harris Bank was on board to lead a syndicate of banks that included CIBC. The facility was also contingent on completion of a high-yield bond issue. Wells Fargo and BMO led a road show that involved about a hundred presentations across the United States and Canada to institutions familiar with the subprime sector. We asked for US$300 million, but with the order book swelling to more than three times that amount, we were able to raise the high-yield issue to US$325 million. The 2017 bank facility was approved for CA$110 million with an accordion feature (an option that gives a company the right to increase its line of credit) for an additional CA$75 million. We completed another bond issue in July 2018, raising US$150 million at an interest rate of 7.86 per cent, followed by a bought deal in October 2018 that injected another CA$46 million in fresh equity.

BMO Nesbitt Burns also became a financial advisor to goeasy. Since I was on BMO's payroll throughout the time of my involvement with RTO, easyhome, and goeasy, I dealt with the potential conflict of interest by excusing myself from any decisions on retaining BMO Nesbitt Burns as a financial advisor.

Another big step forward for goeasy came in 2018, when the board approved a succession plan for top management. Jason Mullins, who had been instrumental in the recent expansion, took over as president and chief executive in January 2019, while David—still only fifty-two years old—moved into the role of executive chair. I became chair emeritus. This time, the transition was well organized and smoothly executed, as it took place over two years. I have no doubt that the company is now well positioned for long-term success and stability, a belief that many others apparently share, judging by the surging share price.

What a ride it has been, spanning almost two decades. The company value was just under $10 million and now trades well over $1 billion. The Toronto Stock Exchange ranked goeasy among its thirty best share-price performers over the three years from 2016 to 2018, and the September 2019 *Report on Business* named it one of Canada's fastest growing companies based on revenue growth. I have a list of friends and colleagues who have invested in goeasy, some buying as many as fifty thousand or one hundred thousand shares. I'm pleased to say that goeasy's success has helped them forgive me for my earlier misguided advice on Rentown.

And despite the ups and downs in our relationship, I'm grateful to my nephew Gord. It all started with him those many years ago. Had I not taken that call from Murray Sinclair and invested in Rentown, we would almost certainly not be where we are today. What's more, if Rentown or RTO Enterprises had flourished, I would probably have earned only a relatively small return on my investment. There would have been no reason for me to replace the directors, nor to hire David Ingram as CEO. As things have turned out, goeasy is by far the best investment I have made in my life. It's an amazing success story—and I'm confident that the best is yet to come.

CHAPTER 6

BETTER TO GIVE
WITH A WARM HAND
THAN A COLD HAND

A series of events during 1984, the year before I reached my half-century, opened my eyes to the world of philanthropy. Yes, I had long understood that we are morally obligated, to the extent we are able, to contribute time or money for the greater good. My mother always helped those in need in our hometown of Lundar and did the same after we moved to Winnipeg. She could not afford to give money; instead, she donated her time to help many of our neighbours in need. But it took me until 1984, four years after her death, to start emulating her example.

I'd just been appointed president of Burns Fry, and I was eager to do the best job I could. To that end, I was really keen to meet John Whitehead, who was co-chairman of Goldman Sachs, one of Wall Street's most storied and respected investment banks. Goldman was the kind of company I wanted Burns Fry to be. One of its hallmarks was a partnership culture, which meant that its top managers always put the interests of clients first, and the interests of fellow partners ahead of their own. I made a cold call to John shortly after I took over as president, asking for a brief meeting so I could seek his advice on how to replicate the Goldman culture in Toronto. To my surprise, he took my call

83

and agreed to meet in his New York office two days later. I had asked to spend fifteen to twenty minutes with him, but we ended up talking for a full hour and a half.

I asked John to tell me about his management philosophy and how he divided his time as co-chairman. The message that really registered with me was that he divided his days into three main segments: one-third for management, one-third for corporate and government clients, and the remaining one-third as a volunteer board member of charities and other not-for-profit groups. He told me that the time he spent in each of the three areas gave a real lift to his role in the other two. I asked how his time in the philanthropic sector could possibly benefit his role in management and with Goldman's clients. I will always remember him saying that as a volunteer board member of charitable organizations, he'd had the chance to meet some very interesting senior executives in a wide variety of industries, and that he'd learned a lot about their management philosophies. He told me he had developed close relationships with a number of these executives— and that some had even signed on as Goldman clients.

Shortly after that meeting, Anna and I were invited to a Christmas party, where I got chatting with our friend Liz Tory, a keen volunteer and philanthropist and the mother of current Toronto mayor John Tory (who at the time was principal secretary to Ontario Premier Bill Davis). I told Liz that I wanted to get involved in a worthwhile cause, and wondered how to go about choosing the right one. She knew that my eyesight wasn't great, and told me of her work with an eye-related charity. She mentioned Dr. Bill Callahan, an ophthalmologist who was in the process of setting up an organization to conduct research into the causes and prevention of various eye disorders. Dr. Callahan had met with

Premier Davis and John Tory to share his dream, and later convinced them to help fund it. The Eye Research Institute of Ontario, affiliated with the University of Toronto and Toronto Western Hospital, opened in 1984, and the Ontario government provided it with a $4.5-million research grant in 1987. While these funds were enough to get the institute off the ground, Dr. Callahan needed to raise more capital to attract researchers and cover operating expenses. Liz wondered whether I would like to get together with her and Dr. Callahan to talk about his work. I immediately agreed.

The upshot of the meeting was that I agreed to chair a fundraising campaign for the institute. Inspired by John Whitehead, I had found an opportunity to get involved in an area of philanthropy that I felt passionate about. As the institute did not have any full-time staff to assist me, we obviously needed to retain the services of an outside agency with the resources and expertise to organize the campaign. We ended up engaging Ketchum Canada, a fundraising consultancy headed by Ross McGregor.

Shortly after Ketchum came on board, Anna and I flew off on a two-week vacation to Nassau in the Bahamas. I had intended to focus on the fundraising campaign when we returned. However, no sooner was I back in the office than Ketchum greeted me with the news that Dr. Callahan—who, I had learned, was not an easy man at the best of times—had terminated the agency's contract on the grounds that the institute could not afford its services. To my surprise and disappointment, he had not discussed this move with me at all. I felt I had little choice but to step down immediately as campaign chair. There was no way I could lead a successful campaign without the benefit of Ketchum's expertise and support, and I was confident that whatever the agency charged would be recouped many times over in donations.

Fortunately, the board saw my point. It called a special meeting and asked Dr. Callahan to step down as chair of the Eye Research Institute of Ontario. Dr. Robert Mitchell, husband of Barbara Mitchell, whose brother Galen Weston was the scion of the Weston food and retail empire, took over as chair of the Institute in 1992. He invited me to join the board and resume my stewardship of the fundraising campaign, with a promise that the institute would hire Ketchum after all. I was delighted to be back in the saddle. Among those I approached for donations was media baron Conrad Black. "It could be called the Black Eye Institute," I joked. Conrad laughed, but took a pass. He was already a donor to Toronto Western Hospital, and did later direct some of his contributions to the Eye Institute.[18]

Around that time, we changed the institute's name from the Eye Research Institute of Ontario to the Eye Research Institute of Canada (ERIC) so that we could appeal to potential donors across the country, rather than in just one province. But I realized early on that I had a lot to learn about philanthropy, and especially fundraising. In order to deepen my knowledge, I decided to visit some of the top eye hospitals in the United States to see how they conducted their campaigns. My trip took me to the Jules Stein Eye Institute in Los Angeles, the Bascom Palmer Eye Institute in Miami, and the Wilmer Eye Institute at the Johns Hopkins Hospital in Baltimore. The key takeaway from all of them was that we should focus our fundraising efforts on grateful, wealthy patients, or, in the pithy words of one of their executives: "rich guys with bad eyes."

Back in Toronto, I arranged to meet with some of the ophthalmology specialists at Toronto Western Hospital, with which ERIC was affiliated, with a view to approaching their grateful, wealthy patients. As it turned out, the doctors were doing their own fundraising for clinical research and for the latest diagnostic equipment, and they politely but firmly refused to give us access to their patient lists. We came up with a better solution by arranging for ERIC to merge in 1999 with Toronto Western's research division. This gave us access to the hospital's ophthalmological resources, including its patients, and the ability to raise funds for vision research. As part of the merger, I joined the board of the Toronto General & Western Hospital Foundation, but with the condition that my fundraising activities would focus on eye research. We then formed a "vision campaign cabinet" of people with an interest in the cause and good contacts with "rich guys with bad eyes."

Meanwhile, we had received a boost a year earlier when John Stevens, ERIC's executive director, set up a company called Visible Genetics, which he took public in late 1996. Because ERIC had helped create the company, it could justifiably lay claim to half of its intellectual property, valued at $5.75 million. Rather than simply transfer $5.75 million worth of Visible Genetics shares to the University of Toronto, Dr. Arnie Aberman, dean of the faculty of medicine, arranged for John Stevens to donate the shares to the University of Toronto in 1999 to fund a new Vision Science Research Program. The program provides funding to this day for students and professors in the U of T's department of ophthalmology to use ERIC's facilities for their research. It has helped more than one hundred and fifty students since 2000. On top of that, the $5.75 million donation was matched by surplus funds from the University of Toronto's Ontario Student Opportunity Trust Funds Awards and by the Ontario government, raising the Vision Science endowment fund, according to the program, to a hefty $17.25 million. The fund continues to distribute about 3.5 per cent of its assets each year for research at ERIC, which is still based at Toronto Western.

The board periodically hosted meetings between the vision campaign cabinet and senior institute staff. At one such get-together, we discussed recruiting new talent for the institute, and in particular, a top researcher from the University of California, Dr. John Flannery.

Dr. Flannery had received an offer shortly before our approach to take a prestigious position at the University of British Columbia. At our next campaign cabinet meeting, I suggested that we could perhaps persuade him to join us instead by putting up $5 million for our eye institute and inviting him to lead it. All agreed this would be a smart move, so our team contacted U of T and Toronto Western Hospital to see if they could come up with the money. Unfortunately, they would not.

This setback turned out to be the catalyst for my decision in 2007 to donate $5 million ($1 million per year over five years) to the research division at Toronto Western, and simultaneously make an offer to Dr. Flannery to move to Toronto and lead the research team at what would be renamed the Donald K. Johnson Eye Centre. It seemed like a once-in-a-lifetime opportunity to contribute to a great cause dear to my heart, and I was fortunate enough to own shares that had appreciated sufficiently to enable me to fulfill the pledge. (I always make my donations in shares and never in cash, because donating shares is more tax effective.) John Flannery eagerly accepted our offer, but said it would take a year or two before he could make the move to Toronto.

Alas, the story did not end there. It took longer than expected to secure lab space for Dr. Flannery, refurbish it, and buy the necessary equipment. By 2009, he was spending about half of his time in Toronto. But we were taken aback the following year, when he informed us that he could no longer accept our offer and would be staying put in Berkeley. I was very disappointed, but at least the institute had my $5-million donation.

Realizing there was nothing we could do to keep Dr. Flannery, we set up a search committee to recruit a new head of research. It took a while, but we were very fortunate in 2013 to find Dr. Valerie Wallace, a senior scientist and director of the Vision Research Program at the Ottawa Hospital Research Institute. Valerie had built a stellar reputation in Ottawa over the previous fifteen years, and we were delighted that she was willing to move to Toronto to take the job.

To mark my eightieth birthday in June 2015, I pledged another $10 million to Toronto Western—two-thirds for basic research and one-third for clinical research at the eye centre. This amazing combination of laboratory and clinic is now named the Donald K. Johnson Eye Institute, a division of the Krembil Neuroscience Centre, and is led jointly by Valerie Wallace, who is still head of research, and Dr. Robert Devenyi, ophthalmologist-in-chief. It is an immense honour to know that an institute with my name above the door is recognized as Canada's leading eye health centre and one of the top five in North America. The Institute has about eighty-five thousand patient visits each year for people with a variety of everyday and complex eye disorders.[19]

The institute's research scientists interact frequently with clinical ophthalmologists so they can obtain access to patient material for research. This collaboration helps researchers gain a better understanding of the causes of eye disease, while enabling clinicians to identify suitable case studies for research, leading in time to the development of effective treatments, and even cures. The institute also conducts clinical trials for promising medications to treat various eye diseases. Its ophthalmologists treat glaucoma and all aspects of retinal disease, including macular degeneration, diabetic retinopathy, retinal detachment, severe ocular trauma, ocular infection, and disease of the cornea. I'm especially proud that it has become the world leader in retinal and corneal surgery.

■ ■ ■

My advocacy campaign for wider tax relief on charity donations, described in detail in the next chapter, dates back to 1995. The proposal to remove the capital gains tax on donations of listed securities was initially designed to boost our campaign for the National Ballet of Canada. But every charity in the country—no matter who it helps and no matter its size—could be a winner if this measure were adopted. I have continued to plead the case for this adjustment in our tax rules as often as I can before the House of Commons Standing Committee on Finance during its annual pre-budget consultation hearings. Rather than speaking solely as a director of the National Ballet, I now feel that my wider philanthropic interests put me in a position to represent a broad cross-section of the charitable sector.

I have also had the pleasure and privilege over the years to be a volunteer board member of several prominent not-for-profit groups. In 1996, Hal Jackman, then chair of the Council for Business and the Arts (now known as Business and Arts) invited me to join that organization's board. It was an honour to accept, partly because Hal was a good friend, but also because my wife, Anna, had a life-long passion for the arts, particularly ballet. In 1997, I joined the advisory board of Ivey Business School at Western University, where I received my MBA in 1963.

As a way of broadening my philanthropic activities, I did some research into charities that support those in need and concluded that the United Way offered the most effective way of helping the disadvantaged. United Way Greater Toronto provides funding for about 270 social service agencies across the region. The agency gave me a "stewardship call" in 1998, asking me to help with its major gift planning. Five years later, I was invited to join its major individual giving cabinet, and I've been a member of that blue-ribbon group ever since. Finally, joining the board of the Toronto General & Western Hospital Foundation in 1999 rounded off my involvement in the non-profit sector. Besides the arts, education, social services, and health, I have taken a keen interest in a wide spectrum of other good causes. It has been a pleasure to donate to such diverse charities as Imagine Canada, Grace Church on-the-Hill in Toronto, Winnipeg's Assiniboine Park Conservancy, and Habitat for Humanity.

Volunteering as a board member at several of these organizations has been a rewarding experience over the past twenty-plus years. I have had the opportunity to meet a great number of interesting leaders from a wide variety of backgrounds. Our conversations have given me a deep appreciation for the vital role that not-for-profit groups play in providing essential, often life-changing, services to all Canadians. I have also learned the valuable role that volunteer boards play in providing advice and counsel to these groups, and in fundraising for their good works. I'm reminded at each board meeting of the importance of giving something back to the communities that have contributed so much to whatever success we have achieved in our lives.

It also gives me a great deal of satisfaction to see the tangible difference that my donations have made to the work of each of these charities. Nowhere is this clearer than at the Eye Institute, which now has the resources to attract and retain star researchers focusing on the causes and treatment of glaucoma, cataracts, macular degeneration, and other eye diseases. The donations have enabled the institute to acquire the latest technology and equipment for researchers and clinicians, and to launch a clinical trials program for new medications to treat eye diseases. What's more, I've been able to introduce a number of people to specialists at the institute for some of the best treatment anywhere in the world.

I have had my own share of eye problems, including high myopia, glaucoma, cataracts, and early age-related macular degeneration. Glaucoma has restricted the peripheral vision in both my eyes, and I would have lost my central vision had it not been treated. Cataracts clouded my eye lenses, making it harder to read, drive (especially at night), and see others' facial expressions. But I've been fortunate to be treated by a superb team of doctors at the Donald K. Johnson Eye Institute, including Rob Devenyi, Graham Trope, and Allan Slomovic. The results have been amazing: at the time of writing in early 2020, I have excellent vision without glasses for the first time in my life. At the age of eighty-four, I need glasses only for reading.

Likewise, my work with the National Ballet of Canada has brought immense pleasure. If Anna had not made her career as a ballet dancer and teacher, I probably would not have been invited onto the ballet company's board. It has been a most rewarding relationship. Chairing the company's Bold Steps campaign in 1995 was the catalyst for our advocacy campaign on charitable donations. We raised $13 million ($1 million more than the original goal), enough to build a wonderful new building on Queens Quay in Toronto that houses rehearsal spaces and the National Ballet headquarters. Called the Walter Carsen Centre, after the businessman who was the lead donor for the centre, it opened in 1996.

Our advocacy drive might never have gotten off the ground had Jim Pitblado, a friend and former chairman of RBC Dominion Securities, and Karen Kain, perhaps Canada's greatest ballerina, not convinced me to chair the Bold Steps campaign. The company honoured Karen in 2019 for fifty years of excellence as an artist and leader by setting up the Karen Kain Legacy Fund, which recognizes her role in leading the National Ballet to new heights and will help to ensure that the company remains a leading light in the artistic world both in Canada and internationally. (Dear Reader: please consider donating to the fund!)

I have also found great satisfaction in being a member of United Way Toronto's major individual giving cabinet since the early 2000s. The catalyst for my most important contribution to United Way came in 2005, when Tony Fell, honorary chair of United Way of Greater Toronto and former chairman of RBC Capital Markets, and Frances Lankin, then United Way Toronto's president and CEO, visited my office to share a groundbreaking report, *Poverty by Postal Code*, and a new strategy, known as *Building Strong Neighbourhoods*. The strategy recognized that many inner-suburb neighbourhoods lacked the social infrastructure to provide services to local residents. It proposed setting up a series of community hubs that would bring residents and service providers together by offering a variety of programs to meet the community's needs—including those of newcomers, seniors, parents, people seeking work, youth, the mentally ill, and others with health problems. The centres would also be a venue for discussions, recreation, and other community activities, such as cooking. Tony and Frances explained the thinking behind the plan, and asked if I could help. It was impossible to say no to two such great community leaders, and I was delighted to pledge $1 million over five years to get the first hub up and running in Scarborough. It opened in December 2009. After that, I chipped in another $300,000 over four years for a second hub on Jane Street, in the west end of the city.

On the education front, the MBA degree that I earned in 1963 was a game changer in my career, enabling me to make the transition from engineering to financial services and investment banking. It also turned out to be another catalyst for deeper involvement in philanthropy. I wanted to give back to Western University's Ivey Business School as a member of the advisory board and through personal donations, and have been happy to donate a total of $4.2 million to the school. I was surprised, honoured, and humbled when the interim dean told me in late 2018 that Ivey was proposing to rename its Toronto campus at First Canadian Place the Donald K. Johnson Centre.

By giving, I have also received—not money, but friendship, kindness, and gratitude, all of which have greatly enriched my life. Allan Slomovic, one of those skilled specialists at the Eye Institute, was generous enough to put it this way:

Don Johnson is one of those larger-than-life individuals that you meet if you are lucky during your lifetime. His favourite expression typifies everything that makes him so special: "it is better to give with a warm hand than a cold hand." Diving deeper you see the warmth, compassion, and the energy driving Don. He wants to leave this world a better place. He certainly leaves a lasting impression and example for those who have the good fortune of interacting with him.[20]

I often think back to where it all started: that meeting with John Whitehead at Goldman Sachs in 1984. John and I remained friends until he passed away at the age of ninety-two, in 2015. After he retired from Goldman twenty years earlier, I made a point of trying to meet him each November when Anna and I made our annual pre-Christmas trek to New York to reconnect with friends, attend theatre events, and do some Christmas shopping. Our last meeting was in November 2014, just a couple of months before he died. John was well aware that he had been the role model for my philanthropic work, and that seemed to give him a good deal of pleasure. He was a wise and inspirational man, and I miss him still.

CHAPTER 7

THE SALE BEGINS WHEN THE CUSTOMER SAYS *NO*

For the past twenty-five years, I've been fighting to change our tax laws to make them more effective in stimulating charitable giving. Our advocacy campaign has already scored one major victory: Canadians can now make donations of public stocks without paying any capital gains tax. But that victory didn't come easily. And now we're working hard on another campaign for change.

The seeds of my crusade were planted in 1993, when I was vice-chairman of investment banking at Burns Fry. That's when Jim Pitblado, who chaired the National Ballet of Canada, came to visit me at my office and invited me to join the board. I knew Jim because he was a fellow Manitoban and had been a great competitor of ours as chairman of RBC Dominion Securities. He knew that I might have an interest in the National Ballet because my wife, Anna, was the artistic director of the Interplay School of Dance, a ballet academy she founded in 1983. I had no hesitation in accepting Jim's invitation.

One year later, Jim and Larry Heisey, the former president and chair of Harlequin Enterprises who was also on the ballet company's board, visited me at my office accompanied by the famous ballerina Karen Kain. "We plan to build a new home for the National Ballet of Canada on Queens Quay here in Toronto,"

Jim told me. They needed to raise $12 million for the complex and suggested that I chair the fundraising campaign, known as Bold Steps. It was impossible to say no to Jim, Karen, and Larry, a formidable trio for whom I had huge respect.

One of my first moves after taking up the challenge was to call a friend in New York who had a wealth of experience in fundraising, especially for his alma mater, Harvard Business School. I asked him if he had any advice for our campaign. "Keep two things in mind," he said. "First, focus on people who love ballet. Second, get them to give stock as an alternative to cash."

I shared my friend's advice with members of our campaign cabinet, one of whom was Ron Gage, the head of Ernst & Young in Canada. Ron invited his tax partner, Satya Poddar, into our meeting to discuss the tax implications of my friend's suggestions. Satya had spent several years at the Department of Finance in Ottawa, so he was an expert on this subject. He told us that when anyone in Canada donated shares to a charity, the donor was deemed for tax purposes to have sold the shares, triggering capital gains tax on the gift. Yes, there was the charitable donation tax credit, but the capital gains tax offset a significant portion of that—with the result that virtually no one was donating stock to charities in Canada at that time.

I immediately called my friend in New York and told him that, unfortunately, his idea would probably not fly north of the border. Undeterred, he reminded me that in the United States, gifts of appreciated capital property were exempt from capital gains taxes. These gifts included listed securities, private company shares, and real estate.

The US system made so much sense. Why couldn't Canada have the same tax treatment on such donations? Taking my own situation, a significant portion of my assets were in the form of equities. I would really have liked to be able to donate some of these investments to my favourite charities, and then the charity could sell them and use the cash proceeds to finance its good deeds. But at that time, our tax treatment was a barrier to any such generosity. Surely, I thought, there must be many other people like me who would love to donate stock if they didn't have to pay a capital gains tax on their gift? Changing this policy would be a win-win.

Over dinner that night, I told Anna what I had learned, and she suggested that this could be a real opportunity to transform philanthropy in Canada. She was right, and I resolved to take up the cause. The first step was to call a special campaign cabinet meeting to tell our members about the difference between American and Canadian rules on the tax treatment of donations of appreciated capital property. Like me, the rest of the team felt strongly that a change was needed. And so we launched our campaign to persuade the government to amend the Income Tax Act and exempt donations of listed securities from capital gains taxes.

I contacted Jim Peterson, a friend who was the Liberal MP for Willowdale in north Toronto and chair of the House of Commons Standing Committee on Finance. Even he was not aware of the difference in the tax treatment of donations in the US and Canada. I also reached out to two former finance ministers, Donald Macdonald and John Turner—and they, too, were unaware of the difference. Jim suggested that I appear as a witness before his committee during its pre-budget consultation hearings in the fall of 1995.

So, on a cool autumn day, I sat before the committee in the Centre Block of Parliament Hill as a board member of the

National Ballet of Canada and made our pitch: that the committee should recommend that the government amend the Income Tax Act to remove the capital gains tax on charitable donations of appreciated property.

Even though I was officially representing only the National Ballet, our intervention seemed to make a mark. The finance committee's 1996 report noted:

> In its report last year, the committee recommended that appreciated capital property donated to charitable organizations be exempted from capital gains taxation. Its chief advocate, Donald K. Johnson, appeared before our committee this year, again advocating this approach. He was supported by many representatives of charities involved in health care, education, social services and the arts.[21]

Even so, for reasons that remain a mystery to me, the 1996 budget made no mention of an exemption. I did get the impression, however, when I followed up with committee members later, that many of them simply didn't have much interest in the well-being of the National Ballet.

But I wasn't ready to give up. In order to try again, we had to figure out why our first pitch hadn't captured the interest of the committee. Some quick research revealed that only about 10 to 15 per cent of charitable donations went to arts and culture. Health care, education, and social services received a much larger share. This was good to know; perhaps we could get the attention of the finance committee during its next pre-budget consultations, coming in the fall of 1996, if we included those other sectors in our pitch.

In preparation for that campaign, we assembled a group of senior representatives of hospitals, universities, social service agencies, and arts and cultural groups, so that this time we'd have someone to speak on behalf of each area of the not-for-profit sector. They included Jim Pitblado, chair of Toronto's SickKids hospital; Rob Prichard, president of the University of Toronto; Robin Cardozo, vice-president and chief executive of United Way of Canada; and Hal Jackman, who was there as the Lieutenant-Governor of Ontario but who also chaired the Council for Business and the Arts (now known as Business and Arts).

What a difference they made! One year after I had appeared alone in front of the House finance committee, each of these leaders came to Ottawa to hammer home the need for extra funding from the private sector. They also made the valid point that the federal government was focused at the time on returning to a balanced budget so charities could not realistically expect any more government support for their vital work. It was clear that we now had the committee's attention. And sure enough, our proposal was among the committee's recommendations for the 1997 budget in its report to the full House of Commons. As Jim Peterson would later observe, these people were so compelling that we were finally able to break the log-jam in Ottawa.

But we still faced an important group of skeptics in the form of senior bureaucrats in the finance department. They were concerned that further tax relief on charitable donations would cost the treasury hundreds of millions of dollars in lost revenues at a time when the government was facing huge deficits. They also believed that the government, not the donor, should decide which not-for-profit groups should benefit from taxpayer funding. We needed to find a way of getting around that opposition.

I wondered if there was anything our team could do to make the proposal palatable enough to persuade the naysayers that it would be worth including in the government's next budget, due to be presented in early 1997. A good friend who had spent many years in federal politics and knew his way around Ottawa came up with some excellent advice: "Don, you need to have a grassroots campaign." He said the best way to win the support of MPs and senators would be to educate them on the benefits of our proposal with the help of business and community leaders in their constituencies who might sway them in our direction.

So we got busy. We wrote a personal letter to each MP and senator outlining the benefits of our proposal for not-for-profit groups, not only in their own constituencies but also across Canada. The letter was just one page long and typed on my personal letterhead; I personally signed each one. The letter asked the recipient to raise this important public policy issue in upcoming caucus meetings to help ensure that Minister of Finance Paul Martin and Prime Minister Jean Chrétien were aware of just how much public support our proposal had. I also listed the concerns expressed by the Department of Finance and provided a response to each.

It was a very busy time, and we had to be relentless. Jim Peterson recalled recently an incident from that time that proved to him how tenacious I could be, and how serious I was about pushing for this change. I showed up at his house at 10 a.m. on a Sunday morning. We had been working together on this issue for a while at that point. I parked in his driveway and then called him from the car. When he answered, I said, "I've got to see you." He asked me when, and I said, "How about right now?" Of course, he was only too pleased to oblige.

To our delight, the 1997 budget cut the capital gains tax payable on a gift of securities in half. The change initially applied for only five years, but became permanent in 2002. I was at Parliament Hill in Ottawa to witness the budget speech first-hand, and the words on page 114 of the background document were music to my ears: "This substantial reduction in the income inclusion rate will facilitate the transfer of capital to charities ... Canadian charities now have a powerful set of tools for raising the funds they need to meet the needs of Canadians."[22] Afterwards, I called Jim, Rob, Robin, and Hal to share the good news with them.

Paul Martin and Jean Chrétien were able to push through the change because they had the support of their MPs and other stakeholders, reinforced by our letter-writing campaign. To his credit, the finance minister made the decision that was best for all charities across Canada and all Canadians who benefit from their vital services. I told him as much when I met him in his office in Ottawa and thanked him. Cutting the capital gains tax on stock donations is simply good public policy.

Our advocacy campaign wasn't over yet. Indeed, we would not rest until the government had finished the job, and removed capital gains tax entirely from gifts of listed securities. So every year that I could after 1997, I made the trek to Ottawa to appear before the Standing Committee on Finance during its pre-budget consultation hearings. I also wrote to a list we'd assembled over the years of more than seven hundred volunteer board members of not-for-profit organizations across the country. I urged each of them to meet with their local MP to explain how our proposal could benefit the needy in their communities.

I like to think that I gained more credibility on Parliament Hill as I expanded my own philanthropic connections. Over the next few years, I joined the advisory board of the Ivey Business School at Western University, my alma mater; the board of the Toronto General & Western Hospital Foundation; the board of Business for the Arts; and became a member of the major individual giving cabinet of United Way of Greater Toronto. These positions not only gave me a good deal of pleasure but also meant that I could speak with more authority because, beyond the National Ballet, I was now deeply involved in health care, post-secondary education, and social services. Ross McGregor, a founding principal of Ketchum Canada, the fundraising consultancy I had worked with at the Eye Institute, was kind enough to offer these thoughts on my work: "Donald Johnson was a tenacious advocate for changes in the Canadian tax regime and other measures to strengthen philanthropy in this country."[23]

I also met with the heads of some non-profit umbrella groups to gauge their interest in supporting my campaign. However, because each of these organizations was making its own pitches on other matters to the House finance committee, my team and I were concerned that *our* key message—eliminating the capital gains tax on gifts of stock—would be diluted if tucked into a package of other, unrelated proposals.

We made sure to keep all the main political parties in the loop. The New Democratic Party was opposed because it perceived our proposal as a "tax break for the rich." However, we kept in touch with five former NDP politicians who came to recognize the benefits of the measure after they became involved in the not-for-profit sector. One was Bob Rae, who became chairman of the Toronto Symphony Orchestra a few years after his tumultuous term as premier of Ontario. The orchestra was in financial trouble, but a substantial amount of money flowed into its coffers from donations of shares after the capital gains tax was cut in half in 1997. Removing the rest of the capital gains tax on gifts of stock would surely stimulate even more donations from the orchestra's many well-heeled supporters.

Bob Rae had this to say about my work:

> I have known Don for many years. Don's campaign was well focused and remarkably persistent. He's done a remarkable job. When I became chair of both the Royal Conservatory of Music and the TSO, my view was that since governments on their own were not prepared to provide more direct funding, the next best recourse was to provide a bigger incentive for charitable giving. I endorsed Don's proposal and was glad to do so.[24]

We then got in touch with Frances Lankin, who had been a cabinet minister in the Rae government and was by then president of United Way of Greater Toronto. She agreed with us that more donations of shares would be a real bonanza. She commissioned an analysis of share donations to the United Way since its inception in 1956. It found that in the forty years from 1956 to 1996, total donations of shares amounted to only $44,000. But in the eight years since 1997, when the capital gains tax was halved, gifts of stock had surged to more than $24 million. That was a massive boost, and one that Frances was eager to continue, and enhance. I also discussed the issue with Anne Swarbrick, another former minister in the Rae government. She headed the Toronto Community Foundation and recognized the importance of share donations to similar agencies across Canada.

Next on my lobbying list was David Miller, then Toronto's mayor. We discussed the fact that hospitals, universities, social service agencies, and arts and cultural groups across the GTA would receive significant extra funding from the private sector if the remaining capital gains tax was removed. I explained that, importantly, there would be no fiscal cost to the city because municipalities derive their revenues primarily from property taxes, not income taxes. In practice, the cost of the measure would be borne about two-thirds by the federal government and one-third by the provinces. David was certainly supportive.

Finally, I contacted Roy Romanow, the former NDP premier of Saskatchewan who had chaired the Commission on the Future of Health Care in Canada. Although he favoured more public financing and ownership of hospitals, he recognized that they were the greatest beneficiaries of these private-sector donations.

I asked each of these former NDP politicians to send me a letter confirming their support. They all agreed. I then forwarded these letters to Jack Layton, then NDP leader, copying Judy Wasylycia-Leis, the NDP finance critic. Imagine how thrilled I was when the two of them wrote back in November 2005 to say that the NDP, too, would throw its weight behind the proposal.

The Bloc Québécois had consistently supported the initiative. So now it was time to talk to the Conservatives. In November 2005, Stephen Harper, who had been elected party leader a year earlier, was the guest speaker at a Canadian Club lunch at the Sheraton Centre in Toronto. I was a director of the club, and I made a point of attending the speaker's reception prior to the event. I immediately contacted the future prime minister and wasted no time broaching my favourite subject.

"When you were leader of the Reform Party," I reminded him, "you were definitely supportive of our measure." He replied that perhaps the Conservatives should include it in their election platform. I certainly wasn't going to argue with that. But I did wonder over the next weeks whether he'd taken our conversation to heart.

I need not have worried. Sure enough, the Conservative election platform in January 2006 contained this item:

> *Supporting charitable giving: Charities play an invaluable role in helping other Canadians and building our sense of community. Government should make it easier for Canadians to support the charities of their choice.*
> *The plan*
> *A Conservative government will:*
> - *Remove the capital gains tax on listed stocks donated to charities. Government should not penalize Canadians when they contribute to charities. Canadians who donate publicly traded shares to Canadian charities should not pay capital gains taxes on those donations.*[25]

I then made a call to Karl Littler, a senior tax policy advisor to Paul Martin, who by then was prime minister. I told him that the Conservatives had included our measure in their election platform and that the NDP and Bloc Québécois were also onside. Furthermore, we had the backing of all major stakeholders in the not-for-profit sector across Canada, and I had no doubt that our proposal would also resonate with many voters. Karl said he would call Minister of Finance Ralph Goodale and bring my request to his attention.

Another victory: In late January 2006, one day before the general election, Mr. Goodale issued a press release pledging that the Liberal Party, if re-elected, would remove the remaining capital gains tax on gifts of listed securities in its first budget.[26] We were clearly on a roll.

The February 2006 election resulted in the Conservatives forming a minority government, with Jim Flaherty as finance minister. I immediately sent a letter to Mr. Flaherty and to Prime Minister Harper reminding them of their election promise. Equally important, the Liberals, the NDP, and the Bloc Québécois were all supportive, which meant there was no way that they would oppose the measure if it was included in the Conservatives' first budget.

Sure enough, the May 2006 budget included a provision removing the remaining capital gains tax on donations of publicly listed shares. Leaders in the not-for-profit sector across Canada were delighted. After a decade of hard work, our campaign had paid off.

The results have been both impressive and heartwarming. Almost every year since 2006, charities across Canada have received more than $1 billion in gifts of listed securities from individual and corporate donors.

■ ■ ■

The Globe and Mail named me its "nation builder" for 2007.[27] Behind that honour lay a lot of hard work and a real team effort. It could not have happened without the support and contribution of several hundred business and community leaders who vigorously communicated their support to their local Members of Parliament, and to senior politicians and bureaucrats in Ottawa.

Also, some close friends of mine who had experience in the political sector gave me some excellent advice along the way.

But I'm not through with my advocacy on behalf of Canada's charities. There's another breakthrough I'm still aiming for. In 2008, the C.D. Howe Institute, a non-partisan public policy think-tank, hosted a conference at its offices on Yonge Street in Toronto that focused on strengthening charity finance in Canada. The following year the institute invited me to sit on its charities advisory committee, charged with recommending further measures that the government could take to stimulate philanthropy.

Again, we looked at what the United States was doing. There, gifts of appreciated capital property are exempt from capital gains taxes. Such gifts include listed securities, shares in private companies, and real estate. In Canada, we tick just one of those three boxes: the capital gains exemption on gifts of listed securities, thanks to our earlier campaign. So we began urging the government to extend the exemption to gifts of private company shares and real estate.

From 2011 on, I again appeared as often as I could at the House finance committee's pre-budget hearings in the hope of persuading members of the need for this extra change to the Income Tax Act. I resumed the letter-writing campaign that had worked so well in the past, again addressing MPs; senators; and senior bureaucrats in the Prime Minister's Office, the Privy Council Office, and the Department of Finance; as well as hundreds of business and community leaders who serve as volunteer board members.

Things were looking promising in early 2015, and I briefly thought we had achieved another victory. Finance Minister Joe Oliver included just such a measure in his budget in April of that year. Under the provision, if a donor sold private company shares or real estate to an arms-length party and donated the cash proceeds to a registered charity within thirty days, the donor would be exempt from capital gains tax on the donation. Mr. Oliver knew he had the support of the Liberals and the NDP because both Scott Brison, the Liberal finance critic, and NDP leader Thomas Mulcair had publicly supported the change.

Then came a blow. While this measure was included in the budget papers tabled on April 21, it didn't appear in the budget bill that Parliament passed two months later. The proposal to amend the Income Tax Act was unveiled in July of that year, but never went any further. This turned out to be a costly omission for us because the Conservatives were tossed out of office just a few months later, in October 2015. Alas, the incoming Liberal government's first budget, tabled in March 2016, stated explicitly that the new government would not proceed with the measure.

The decision was a surprise and a big disappointment to me and my many friends and supporters in the not-for-profit sector who had worked so hard to give charities access to the extra resources that this amendment would have unlocked. I wrote a passionate opinion piece in *The Globe and Mail* in April 2016 making the case for the Liberals to reconsider. My main points were the following:

- *The demand for services provided by not-for-profit organizations continues to grow, particularly for health care as our population ages, but federal and provincial governments have limited financial capacity. The private sector can help fill this gap. Charitable donations are far more tax-effective than direct government spending.*

- *Our hospitals and universities compete with their US counterparts to attract and retain the smartest doctors, professors, and researchers. Charitable donations often play a key role in providing funding for these talented people. In the US, gifts of appreciated capital property are exempt from capital gains taxes. Removing this barrier would encourage Canadians to donate more, as our per-capita donations are currently just one-half of donations by Americans.*[28]

I couldn't help but wonder what the reason was for the Liberals' backtracking. I asked a lot of questions, meeting with senior bureaucrats at the finance department as well as the policy advisor to the new finance minister, Bill Morneau. Several factors appeared to be at play. Bill Morneau was a first-time Member of Parliament. His first responsibility was to prepare the 2016 budget, but since he had no experience as an MP, let alone as finance minister, he depended even more heavily than his predecessors on his departmental officials to get the job done. But, as I discovered during my earlier campaign, many of them were adamantly opposed to any new incentives for charitable donations. Despite the success of the removal of capital gains tax on stock donations a decade earlier, they had clearly not changed their minds.

It would have been risky for Bill Morneau to go against his department's advice so early in his tenure, despite his previous active involvement in the philanthropic sector. Mr. Morneau had been chairman of St. Michael's Hospital in Toronto and its foundation, as well as a member of its campaign cabinet. He had also served as a director of the Canadian Opera Company as well as chairman of Covenant House Toronto and the C.D. Howe Institute.

Another factor that may have worked against us was that 136 of the 184 Liberal MPs were newcomers to Parliament, so they were probably not even aware of the 2015 budget measure. On top of that, the new Liberal government was determined to reverse many of the special-interest tax cuts that the Conservatives had granted during their decade in office.

Daunting obstacles lie ahead, but I won't give up. As of the fall of 2019, we are working on a fresh campaign to convince the government to reinstate the 2015 budget proposal in its 2020 budget. The annual cost to the treasury of foregone capital gains tax would be only $50 million to $60 million, but I estimate that charities would receive about four times that amount in additional donations each year. Under our proposal, the charitable donation tax credit would be the same as the deduction for cash donations.

It's both humbling and rewarding to hear Marnie Spears, Ketchum Canada's former president and CEO, say:

> *Don has been and continues to be a consistent and ardent advocate on behalf of every one of the changes to personal charitable giving tax, including the most recent in terms of gifts of private shares. He received recognition of his earlier advocacy a number of years ago, in the form of an Association of Fundraising Professionals Volunteer award, and continues to be well known throughout the fundraising profession in Canada as a leading philanthropist who supports not only the causes he and his family care about, but also the greater good of the donor public through his unique volunteer commitment of advocacy.[29]*

I'm honoured that someone who has dedicated her life to philanthropy thinks so well of me. Most of all, I'm happy to have been an agent of change for the better, change that will hopefully spur Canadians to open their pocketbooks and portfolios even wider for the causes that make our world a better place. I've long believed in the importance of giving back—and not waiting too long to do so. As I often say, "It's better to give with a warm hand than a cold hand" or, to put it another way: "He who gives while he lives also knows where it goes."

When people comment on my persistence in this particular campaign, I always respond with one or more of my three favourite philosophies:

1. The sale begins when the customer says no.
2. Persistence prevails when all else fails.
3. Never give up. Never give up. Never, never, never give up!

CHAPTER 8

HBN: HORIZONTAL BY NINE

As I write this in the fall of 2019, my weight—at 160 pounds—is almost exactly the same as it has been for the past forty years. From time to time, people ask me: "Hey, how do you keep so well?" My answer: "Discipline."

Many people in the investment banking business are prone to obesity, high blood pressure, heart problems, and other ailments. The nature of the job means long hours, frequent entertaining, and lots of travelling. But I have always been determined not to let myself go. In fact, I am certain that my relentless focus on staying physically and mentally healthy has made a huge contribution to my happiness and success. I eat right, exercise (a lot), and sleep well—my motto is HBN (Horizontal by Nine), which means I am in bed each night by 9 p.m. As for mental health, the way I keep my stress down and my mind clear may surprise many readers: for five decades, I've been an ardent practitioner of transcendental meditation.

My devotion to TM started in 1968, when I was head of institutional equity sales at Burns Bros. and Denton. I noticed that Frank Mahoney, one of our salesmen in Montreal, had managed to double his commission revenues in just the previous six months. A jump of that magnitude in such a short span of time is almost unheard of in the securities business, especially given that share prices and trading volumes had barely moved, and Frank was still looking after the same roster of institutional clients.

I decided that I should investigate more closely, so I flew to Montreal and invited Frank, a quiet, soft-spoken man, for lunch at Le Caveau restaurant on Rue Victoria, near McGill University. I was in for the surprise of my life. When I asked him about his out-sized commissions, he gave me a cryptic response: "I give full credit to TM." I had never heard that acronym before, so my next question was, "What on earth is TM?"

"Transcendental meditation," he replied.

That also didn't mean much to me, so Frank went on to explain what TM was: a relaxation exercise practised as you sit in a comfortable chair in a quiet, dark room with your eyes closed. The idea is to focus your mind on a mantra—a sound that you repeat to yourself. Done properly, your thoughts then alternate between the mantra and other pleasant things, putting you into a deep state of relaxation. Frank told me that he had learned the technique at a clinic in Montreal, taking ninety-minute classes for four consecutive days.

I then asked him how TM had enabled him to double his commission revenues. First, he said, after practising TM for a few weeks, he was much more relaxed; he could think more clearly and communicate more effectively. He had better judgment and could give his clients more thoughtful advice. His second reason was even more of an eye-opener. It turned out he had recommended TM to three of his clients, who decided to take the same course and were so impressed that they doubled the amount of business they sent his way. Before our lunch even ended, I was hooked.

Transcendental meditation has become an essential part of my daily routine, and over the fifty or so years since I first heard about it, it has helped me appreciate the importance of a healthy lifestyle, regardless of age. My focus on my physical and mental health has been a very important factor in my life. Maintaining a disciplined regimen of exercise, healthy eating habits, sleep, and—not least—TM is still one of my top priorities. More than that, I seldom lose an opportunity to spread my health and fitness message among family, friends, business partners, clients, and even the philanthropic organizations that I work with.

No sooner had I returned home from my visit with Frank than I found a TM instructor near High Park, in the west end of Toronto. I immediately registered and, like Frank, attended four ninety-minute classes. I initially felt a little out of place, as I was the only member of the class who wore a jacket and tie. Most of the others were dressed in blue jeans and sported ponytails. At that time, we would have called them hippies—certainly, they looked a little different from my buttoned-down colleagues on Bay Street. After a few weeks of practise, I started to feel the same benefits that Frank had described. It quickly became clear that two twenty-minute TM sessions a day were a great return on the investment of time. To this day, I often come up with some good ideas during my meditation, and I then make a few handwritten notes afterwards. I find that these sessions give me a great sense of well-being: I'm energized, and actually look forward to getting a lot of things done.

For fifty years now, I have faithfully sat down for a TM session at home each morning before breakfast and again in the late afternoon, either at home or in my office, before dinner. I also meditate when I fly. I wear a noise-cancelling headset to make my environment as quiet as possible. I always practise TM in my hotel room whenever I'm travelling.

It has changed my life. I've discovered that TM is a really effective way of combatting stress, which in turn brings all kinds of other benefits, given the role of stress in weakening our immune system and making us more susceptible to various diseases. Meditation counters the body's stress by triggering relaxation, which can help lower blood pressure, heart rate, breathing rate, oxygen consumption, and levels of the stress hormones adrenaline and cortisone. Research also shows that relaxation may help prevent inflammation[30] and dilate the arteries, leading to lower blood pressure.[31] A TM session before bed each night invariably helps me sleep better. I take the view that it is generally a far healthier option than taking medications with all their side effects. Because the mind and body are closely interconnected, TM can even help alleviate chronic pain. The best evidence I have of its benefits is that I have not been off sick from work a single day in the past fifteen years, and I give TM much of the credit for that.

It helps with mental health, too, a facet of our well-being that has gained a lot of attention in recent years in Canada thanks to some well-known campaigners. Michael Wilson, a former federal finance minister and a dear friend until his death in early 2019, played a key leadership role in addressing the stigma of mental illness and raising the importance of this health challenge across Canada. Considerable research is now being conducted into the causes and treatment of mental illness. TM has been shown to reduce anxiety[32] and depression.[33] My own experience tells me that it encourages positive emotions while helping to push aside destructive ones such as fear and anger. I believe it has also improved my judgment and communication skills, and helped me to come to important decisions on my career and personal relationships.

Based on my personal experience, TM can—and should—play a significant role in many more people's lives. Antidepressants are now prescribed to one in eight adults and adolescents in the United States.[34] One of TM's biggest advantages, I believe, is that it offers a safe, affordable, and even enjoyable alternative to the psychotropic medications so often used to treat mental illness. I have little doubt that if more people practised TM twice a day, some types of mental illness would be dramatically reduced.

For years, I felt a little shy about telling my partners and clients about my interest in TM. I was convinced that they might think I too was turning into a hippie. I always made sure that I did my meditation sessions behind closed doors, and for close to twenty years, I told no one at the office about it. However, I eventually decided that the benefits I had reaped from TM were worth sharing, not only with family but also with friends and business partners. Several of them have since become avid TM fans.

Besides TM, I pay close attention to my diet. I constantly keep an eye on my weight, knowing that the Canadian Cancer Society expects obesity to become the second-leading preventable cause of cancer, after tobacco. I have a scale in my bathroom and weigh myself every day to ensure that I'm not putting on the pounds. It helped that Anna, who maintained the healthy eating habits she learned as a ballerina, showed me by her own example how to be disciplined and weight conscious. I try to stick to whole grains, fruits, vegetables and legumes (especially carrots, broccoli, lentils, and beans), nuts, seeds, and fish high in omega-3 fatty acids. I make sure that I drink seven or eight glasses of water every day, and I avoid processed foods, red meat, and foods with unhealthy trans fats, salt, and sugar. We're learning more and more about the damage that sugar can cause. Unfortunately, most people do not realize that it is a real poison, and an addictive one. The more food you eat or liquids you drink with high sugar content, the more you succumb to sugar cravings. It becomes a vicious cycle that can be very detrimental to your health.

Having said that, it's not always easy to resist temptation. One of the challenges I've found is to identify appropriate foods when eating out, especially in restaurants, and to discipline myself to eat healthy food at home. I've found that the advice of a nutritionist can be invaluable. Fortunately, most restaurants offer at least three alternatives for the main course. I almost always choose fish or chicken, and avoid red meat. When I'm invited to a fundraising event or gala dinner and the coordinator asks me if I have any food allergies or dietary restrictions, my response is that I don't eat red meat. Breakfast is the healthiest meal of my day. I always have it at home, which gives me more leeway to choose what I want to eat, rather than what someone else wants to serve me. I normally enjoy a bowl of high-fibre cereal such as All-Bran Buds or Shredded Wheat, plus a smoothie of flaxseeds, mixed berries, plain yogurt, and soy milk.

And then there's physical fitness. I began to appreciate the importance of exercise a few years ago after reading *Younger Next Year: Live Strong, Fit, and Sexy—Until You're 80 and Beyond,* co-authored by Chris Crowley, a friend who lives in New York, and his doctor friend, Henry S. Lodge. The book makes a compelling case for maintaining an active lifestyle. I've been so impressed by it that I have given away at least a hundred copies to family and friends. The book's main message is that if you want to keep feeling young, you need to exercise six days a week for the rest of your life. Other bits of advice that have resonated with me are to choose the exercises that you enjoy

Anna McCowan Johnson and Don Johnson, 2010.

Close friends Latham Burns and Paddy Ann Burns at Don's home in Toronto, 2010.

Good friends (left to right) Robert Foster, John Campion, and Jean Cumming at Don's home in Toronto, 2010.

Don Johnson with (left to right) Sonja Bata, Nichole Anderson, and Alain Bergeron at Don's home in Toronto, 2010.

Good friends (left to right) Brian Carter, Henri Eschauzier, Latham Burns, and Crawford Gordon at Don's home in Toronto, 2010.

Don Johnson with Tony and Shari Fell at Don's home in Toronto, 2010.

Don beside the outhouse outside their family home in Lundar, Manitoba, 2010.

Don Boxer (left) with Don Johnson in Toronto, 2010.

Don with his siblings in Toronto, 2010 (left to right):
Cy Johnson, Don Johnson, Margret Reykdal, and
Paul Johnson.

David Ingram at the goeasy offices in Mississauga, 2016.
Ingram became chief executive officer of RTO Enterprises
(later goeasy) in 2001, after being recruited by Don Johnson.

David Thomson, Don's good friend since his 1963 MBA program at Western University, in Collingwood, 2017.

David Ingram and Jason Mullins of goeasy accepting the award for the Most Admired Corporate Culture in Canada–Mid-Market from Waterstone Human Capital, Toronto, 2018.

FREQUENTLY WRONG, BUT
NEVER IN DOUBT!

These plaques sit on Don's desk to remind him of the mantras
he tries to abide by in his life and work.

THE SALE BEGINS WHEN THE

CUSTOMER SAYS "NO"!

IT CAN BE DONE

the most, join a gym, and take part in exercise classes. Exercise offers a wealth of benefits. It strengthens your immune system,[35] helps you sleep better,[36] keeps your weight under control,[37] and dramatically lowers the risk of heart disease,[38] stroke,[39] hypertension,[40] Alzheimer's disease,[41] arthritis,[42] diabetes,[43] vascular disease,[44] high cholesterol,[45] and depression.[46]

I'm pretty tough on myself when it comes to exercise. Starting in the late 1960s, I jogged virtually every day, and for several years, I ran five miles each morning, seven days a week. I estimate that over the course of thirty years, I ran about thirty-three thousand miles, or close to one and a half times around the world. Unfortunately, I was forced to scale back a bit in 2000, when I felt some shortness of breath and tightness in my chest while out jogging. I contacted Ted Rogers, who I knew had a close relationship with the famed Mayo Clinic in Rochester, Minnesota, including having quadruple bypass surgery there in 1992. Ted and his GP, Dr. Bernard Gosevitz, put me in touch with Hugh Smith, then chair of Mayo Clinic's Rochester campus and himself a cardiologist, and I met with him two days later.

Hugh and his team conducted extensive tests over two days and concluded that I had a partially blocked artery. However, it was not so badly blocked that I needed bypass surgery, nor was a stent appropriate given the structure of my arteries. Instead, he prescribed medication to address blood pressure and cholesterol levels. He also advised me to give up jogging in favour of working out on an elliptical trainer. That prompted me to build an addition to our house, including a gym with an elliptical trainer. From then on, I worked out three times a week at home, spending thirty minutes each session on the elliptical trainer. On Anna's recommendation, I also started taking Pilates classes twice a week to improve my flexibility, muscle strength, and endurance. Also, I signed up once a week at a gym called Healthy Habits, close to the intersection of Yonge Street and St. Clair Avenue, for exercises that focus on posture, balance, and flexibility. Lastly, I've enjoyed working with a personal trainer who visits me at home once a week for strength training.

For me, a typical week includes about an hour and a half on the elliptical trainer, two Pilates classes, one visit to Healthy Habits, and a visit from my personal trainer. I also walk at least five thousand steps per day, tracked on my Fitbit watch—since walking is such good exercise, that's an additional five hours of exercise per week. My favourites? Pilates classes and my workouts at the Healthy Habits gym. My least favourite thing is the strength training. Now that I no longer have a management role at the office, I have more flexibility in my daily schedule, allowing me to make my health my number-one priority.

Getting enough sleep is also vital. Fifty years ago, most people typically slept for seven or eight hours a night. But today, with heavier demands on our time, and the temptations of new technology—the Internet, mobile devices, social media, and so on—we seem to stay awake far longer. Most people I know now catch only five or six hours sleep a night, often due to heavy workloads.

Researchers at the University of Ferrara in Italy recently studied the link between sleep deprivation and heart attacks.[47] Other studies have confirmed that less than six hours of sleep a night raises the risk of high blood pressure, diabetes, obesity, and even premature death. When we have too little sleep, we tend to eat more calories, but burn fewer of them. Even a single night of disrupted sleep can cause problems.[48]

I had exactly that experience until about ten years ago when I read Stanley Coren's book *Sleep Thieves*. It discusses the impact on our behaviour of the shift to daylight savings time each spring, noting that on the Monday morning after the change, the rate of traffic accidents goes up by about 8 per cent.[49] The reason is that with even one hour of less sleep, drivers do not think as clearly, get distracted, and do not pay close enough attention to the cars in front of or behind them.[50]

The University of Ferrara study concluded that the hour of sleep lost by the switch to daylight savings time each spring has led to a higher incidence of heart attacks on the Monday after the time change, possibly due to a faster heartbeat, elevated blood pressure, higher stress levels, and more of the chemicals that promote inflammation.[51]

After reading all this, I started to reflect on the impact on my health of two fewer hours of sleep every night. I decided to change my sleeping habits, so that instead of going to bed at 10 or 11 p.m. and getting up at 5:30 or 6 a.m., as I used to do, I'm now tucked in by 9:30 p.m. at the latest. (Remember HBN?) I'm convinced that the change has brought about a significant improvement in my general well-being. That extra hour or two of rest enables me to think more clearly and gives me a lot more energy during the day. And going to bed that early is no hardship; we usually have dinner at 5:30 or 6 p.m., whether we are at home or at a restaurant. When attending social events, I like to leave no later than 9 p.m., even if the formal part of the event isn't yet over. I never take a nap, but I frequently do an extra TM session before lunch, which I find equally relaxing and invigorating.

Norman Vincent Peale's seminal book *The Power of Positive Thinking* made a big impact on me when I first read it back in the

1960s. His advice to focus your mind on the positive aspects of whatever life throws at you really struck a chord,[52] and I've taken the view in every challenge that I've faced since then that my glass is half full rather than half empty. Having a positive mental attitude has enhanced my relationships with family, friends, business associates, and even people whom I barely know. In my leadership roles, I've found that it's much easier to assemble and motivate a great team if you focus on their positive attributes, and I've tried to organize management structures so they benefit clients and colleagues.

I can think of at least two occasions when a positive mental attitude helped me through a difficult time. In July 2000, when RTO Enterprises (now goeasy—see Chapter 4) was about to go bankrupt, I managed to persuade four top-notch business leaders to join our board: Douglas Anderson, former president of Thorn Americas (the parent company of Rent-A-Centre); Joseph Rotunda, former chief operating officer of Thorn Americas; Ron Gage, former chief executive of Ernst & Young Canada; and Robin Korthals, former president of TD Bank. My pitch to each of them focused on the opportunity, not the problem. Another stressful time was in 2006, when we were unable to persuade the University of Toronto or the University Health Network to put up the $5 million needed to attract John Flannery, the star researcher from the University of California at Berkeley, to head the new eye institute. Instead of stewing over the setback, I decided to turn it into the catalyst for my initial $5-million donation to the Donald K. Johnson Eye Centre in 2007.

Getting away from the city as much as possible also helps relax my mind. Anna and I started going up to our farm in Caledon, northwest of Toronto, in 1989. It's one of the best investments we ever made in our well-being. Our connection to the farm began on our annual summer vacations in the 1980s at Saint-Paul-de-Vence in the south of France. We often met for lunch or dinner with Richard Holland, a retired judge of the Supreme Court of Ontario, and his family. Richard was also the former president of the Caledon Mountain Trout Club and owned a 76-acre farm nearby. In 1989, he told me he was planning to sell his farm and wondered if I might be interested. Anna and I drove out to take a look, and walking around the property, we quickly fell in love with the house and the spectacular view from the Niagara Escarpment. We figured it would be a wonderful place to spend weekends, especially as it was just a one-hour drive from Toronto, compared to a two- or three-hour trek to a cottage in Muskoka. We bought the property from Dick Holland in 1989.

Going up to the farm—we call it a farm, although we don't keep animals—on weekends is a great way to relax and unwind after five busy days on Bay Street. The view is spectacular, and we have a swimming pool and a tennis court to use during summer weekends. I do like to exercise there, so we recently put on an addition with a gym on the main floor and an office on the second floor. Whenever I'm asked whether I'm planning to retire, my stock response is, "I am starting to slow down. I only go to the office five days a week and the other two days I work from home!" But more and more, I've been taking my work to the farm: board and committee work, and also our charity donations campaign.

Finally, I've always believed in the value of a sense of humour: it's good for the body as well as the mind. None of us should take ourselves too seriously. Laughter is a great stress reliever, and research has shown that it can help boost the immune system. It enhances relationships with all those around us. I practise what I preach: Roger Lomax, the former BAT executive, told me recently that my laugh could be heard around the office even when I was in the elevator. I do enjoy making people laugh—and am known as a bit of a jokester, even at the office. Many times during tense meetings or negotiations, I'd be the one to relieve tension by cracking a joke. It can really help bring the stress level down a few notches.

One pithy expression says it all: laughter is the best medicine. I couldn't agree more!

LOTS TO BE GRATEFUL FOR

I'll close this chapter with some insights into my family life. After separating from my first wife in 1980, I moved into a condominium at 110 Bloor Street West in Toronto. I rented out our old house to a succession of senior provincial politicians, including Darcy McKeough, the former Ontario treasurer, and David Peterson, the former premier.

A year after our separation, my former wife enrolled our two daughters in ballet lessons. As the kids came to stay with me every second weekend, I often took them to their ballet classes, and it didn't take long before I met their teacher, Anna McCowan, the woman with whom I would share my life until her untimely death in August 2020. We began dating, and two years later, in 1983, I moved into Anna's Tudor-style home in Chaplin Estates. We lived together for seven years before marrying in 1990.

Anna had an outstanding career as a dancer and teacher. She studied under Gweneth Lloyd, co-founder of the Royal Winnipeg Ballet, and went on to lead the Interplay School of Dance, one of Toronto's top ballet schools, for more than twenty-three years until she retired in 2006.

Anna's first marriage was to David Gilmour, who was Peter Munk's partner in Clairtone, a stereo maker, and subsequently Peter's partner in South Pacific Hotels, a chain of resorts that started in Fiji. Anna and David divorced in 1963, but Anna kept the beautiful Tudor house in Chaplin Estates. The house was built in 1922 and bought by David's parents in 1939. Anna then married George McCowan, a film producer. They were divorced in the late 1970s, but Anna again stayed put in the house. One of her favourite expressions was: "I change husbands, but I never change houses."

Anna was a great partner over many years. She taught me how to dress properly both for business and for casual events, and always gave me wise advice on the correct etiquette for dining and for hosting receptions and dinner parties. I also became good friends with her two sons, as well as their spouses and children.

While I regret not spending as much quality time as I would have liked with my children when they were growing up, I now enjoy a very close relationship with all three. Each one has followed my advice to do what they love to do, do what they are good at, and be with people they enjoy being with. They have followed their own paths, and I'm very proud of them.

CHAPTER 9

LESSONS LEARNED

You'd hope that anyone would accumulate a wealth of knowledge by the time they reach their mid-eighties, and that's certainly true for me. I have always considered my life experiences to be part of my education. This book is meant to share some of the lessons I've learned along the way ... lessons from my small-town upbringing to finding my way into the world of investment banking, some of the big ups and downs of my fifty-seven years (and counting) on Bay Street and, not least, what I've learned about health and longevity—and people.

WHAT WARREN BUFFETT TAUGHT ME

I've learned a lot from countless people in my network, but one person in my contacts file has taught me more than most: Warren Buffett. Together, we made a real success out of his Home Capital investment. But even in the deals that didn't come together, the lessons I learned were just as valuable:

- I can't emphasize enough how crucial contacts are in the investment banking world. Behind all those business cards are people who connect us to potential deals, and recommend us to their own networks. My network is over six thousand and counting. It's vital to keep up your network, even late in your career.

- If two individuals are to come to a deal, their relationship must embody three essential elements: mutual respect, trust, and confidence. Warren and I were cordial with each other from the start; we treated each other with respect; and we worked together constructively, even if every deal didn't work out.

- The sale begins when the customer says no. I felt no sense of regret when Warren turned down the Suncor investment. Far from it. I knew that I had opened a door to one of the world's most sought-after investors, and was confident that we would explore more opportunities and do business together some day.

- High barriers to entry are a recipe for success. A company has a much greater chance of long-term prosperity if it is in a business where potential rivals cannot easily gain a foothold. Warren coined the term "economic moat," referring to a business's ability to maintain its competitive advantage and, thus, its long-term profit and market share.[53] One of easyfinancial's biggest advantages is protection by just such a moat, given the hurdles that subprime lenders in Canada face in obtaining the financing needed to support their business. easyfinancial's moat certainly meets Warren Buffet's definition, and goeasy has a strong management team in place to capitalize on its strong advantage.

- Persistence prevails when all else fails. After Warren turned down the opportunity to take a stake in Suncor in 1995, I went back to him three times more. Two of the three, Royal and Sun Alliance in 2002 and CP Rail in 2007, didn't work out. But the third, Home Capital, turned out to be a winner. Winston Churchill's words say it all: "Never give in, never give in, never, never, never, never—in nothing, great or small, large or petty—never give in."[54]

BUILD A STURDY FOUNDATION

I'm a small-town boy who had a modest upbringing in Lundar, Manitoba. I wasn't born into money. So the things I learned as a child and as a young man starting a career have turned out to be some of the crucial ingredients to whatever success I have achieved:

- Few things in life are more important than a good education. I would not be where I am today if my mother had not insisted that we move from Lundar to Winnipeg so that I could go to university. In the absence of my dad, my mother was determined to help me succeed. My education was thanks in large part to her hard work and support, starting with the money she earned knitting those socks and mittens for the fishermen on Lake Manitoba.
- Make the sacrifices you need to. I left Toronto, a place I enjoyed, to spend two years in the high Arctic working on the DEW Line. The generous compensation from that job allowed me to pay off my student loans, and I was promoted to manager at the age of just twenty-four. The lifestyle sacrifices were well worth it.
- Make your passion your career. My switch from engineering to investment banking underlined the importance of choosing a career that you love and that you are good at. And do not expect to have your career mapped out when you finish high school. Stay flexible, and try to surround yourself with people whose company you enjoy, both at the office and at

home. If you pick a career that seems to meet these criteria but then find it's not working, move on as quickly as you can, because if you're not happy in a job, chances are you will also not be successful at it. I certainly discovered quite quickly that investment banking had a lot more appeal to me than designing TV sets.

- Look before you leap. Before making a decision, discuss your alternatives with one or two close friends whose judgment you respect. Reflect on the pros and cons of each option after you have heard their advice, and only then make a decision.
- Never forget where you came from. My regular return visits to Lundar with my siblings keep me in touch with my roots and remind me of just how lucky I've been. To be able to give something back to that special community over the years has been such a rewarding experience for me.

FOCUS ON OPPORTUNITIES

I knew very little about the world of investment banking when I joined Burns Bros. and Denton at the age of twenty-eight. I learned many valuable lessons over the next fifty-seven years (and counting) as I rose from an entry-level investment analyst to vice-chair of the firm:

- Have a mentor. When you're starting a new job, especially when you're young, it is helpful to have a mentor who has been with the organization for many years, has extensive experience, and is willing to offer advice to a newcomer. A mentor can be very helpful as a sounding board. I was fortunate to have Don Boxer as my mentor when I joined Burns Bros. and Denton in 1963. He gave me great advice over the years, and we were close friends right up until his death in 2016, at the age of ninety-five. I delivered a eulogy at his funeral.

- No need to be pushy. Tim Beatty, president of Burns Bros. and Denton when I joined, gave me some great advice. He told me to strive to be the best in whatever position I was in, and not to be concerned about promotion because, as he put it, "the cream always rises to the top."

- Be open to change. I knew no one in Montreal when I was transferred there, but I embraced the opportunity to move to a new city and make it my home for a time. The experience taught me a lot about the benefits of going outside your comfort zone. What's more, I made valuable contacts.

- Be flexible; you never know what's around the corner. When the Big Bang hit the UK financial services industry in 1986, Canada quickly followed suit. My colleagues and I had to think fast and be creative, and we managed not only to survive but also to become one of the most-respected firms in the industry.

- Stay focused. The Imasco deal, which closed in early 2000 and left Canada Trust under the wing of TD Bank, was a blockbuster victory for all parties—and it all started when I read a *Financial Times* article on a flight in 1997. I immediately realized the significance of the story, and got the ball rolling with a letter to BAT's chief executive within a day of arriving in London. It goes to show that opportunities can come up anywhere, anytime. It's important to focus on those where you can make a real difference, and which will benefit many people. It took a couple of years to nail down the deal, so I also learned the importance of having the discipline to focus on an opportunity until you are successful, no matter how long it takes.

- Arrange your priorities. I learned this lesson during my first meeting with John Whitehead, the co-chairman of Goldman Sachs, in 1984, shortly after I became president of Burns Fry. We met so that I could learn from Goldman Sachs' partnership culture. John's advice was to put the best interests of your clients first; put the best interests of your partners and shareholders ahead of your own personal interests; and focus on being the best in what you do, rather than looking for a promotion. A decade later, I met Roberto Goizueta, Coca-Cola's CEO at the time. He told me he had a plaque on his desk that read: "There is no limit to what a man can do or where he can go if he doesn't mind who gets the credit."[55] I can't think of a sounder credo to live by.

LEARN FROM YOUR MISTAKES

I learned a great deal from the Rentown financing disaster in 1989. There is nothing more important than your personal reputation and the reputation of your business. It is essential to conduct extensive due diligence on the management and board of directors of a company that requires financial advice *before* doing business with them. When you make a mistake, admit it and make sure you don't make the same mistake again.

Here are some other lessons I've learned about leadership and business relationships:

- Keep family out of decisions on investing and building a business. Such decisions should be based on the attributes of the individuals you are dealing with and should not be swayed by whether they are family members. My nephew's involvement in Rentown and RTO Enterprises was a sobering lesson for me.

- Choose your leader carefully. Nothing is more important to the success of a business than the competence of the chief executive. He or she must have unquestioned integrity and a clear vision for long-term success. The CEO must possess the leadership skills to assemble a strong management team that will implement the corporate strategy. He or she must have a strong desire to succeed, including a willingness to make sometimes-painful personal sacrifices. David Ingram demonstrated all these skills during his eighteen years as CEO of easyhome. The wisest decision that I made as chair was to hire him as the CEO and then stand behind him through thick and thin, especially when Wes Voorheis and his board allies wanted to oust him.

- Be clear on the separate roles of the board and management. The board's mandate is, first and foremost, to ensure that the company has the right chief executive. Then, the directors must provide oversight and advice to management—but they should *not* be involved in managing the company. This was something that Wes Voorheis vehemently disagreed with me on during our time together on easyhome's board—so much so that he tried to oust me as chair in 2011 in order to replace management. The choice of a management team should be left to the CEO, and the new easyhome board in 2012 put this distinction into practice. Indeed, trust and respect between the chair and the chief executive are key to success (or, without them, failure). The chair can play a crucial role in keeping relations between the board and management on an even keel. The close relationship between David Ingram and me was essential in maintaining the delicate balance of roles at easyhome and, subsequently, goeasy.

- Focus on the long term. While many shareholders are fixated on quarterly results, management needs to concentrate on the long-term success of the company—and the board should support that vision. Some decisions that boost short-term performance may not always serve the company's best interests. The management focus at goeasy has always been on the best long-term success.

- Draw up a leadership succession plan. Such a plan is essential to reduce the risk of rivals luring away your most valuable executives, but there is no magic formula. At goeasy, David Ingram, the seasoned chief executive of eighteen years, moved on to become executive chair in order to create room for a younger and highly promising successor, Jason Mullins. The transition was well planned and went very smoothly, with the happy result that, as of fall 2019, goeasy had two top-notch leaders.

Thomas Jefferson's "10 Rules of Life" contain some excellent advice, and not only for those in the business world. Here are three that I have found especially valuable: "Never put off until tomorrow what you can do today ... Never trouble another for what you can do yourself ... When angry, count ten before you speak; if very angry, count a hundred."[56]

THE JOY OF GIVING

I'm so pleased that I sought out John Whitehead at Goldman Sachs in 1984 to ask for his business advice. He inspired me to encourage philanthropy in business and to personally give back, too. Since then, I've learned that good deeds not only help others but also enable you to meet with and learn from other senior executives (who may one day even become clients). But the true joy of giving has come from seeing the tangible results of my philanthropic efforts. The Donald K. Johnson Eye Institute at Toronto Western Hospital, for example, has had the funding to attract star researchers, initiate clinical trials for new medications, and acquire the latest equipment needed to help people suffering from glaucoma, cataracts, macular degeneration, and other eye diseases. More than eighty-five thousand patients visit the institute each year.[57]

These experiences, along with my interactions with fellow members of non-profit boards, have taught me some valuable lessons about fundraising:

- Prospective donors must have a reason to be interested in your cause. Fundraising for a hospital works best when either the donors or their family members or close friends have been patients there. Similarly, when fundraising for a university, the most generous givers are likely those who either graduated from the university themselves or have family who did. The same goes for arts and culture groups—donors are likely to have a passion for some aspect of the arts. In the case of social services, donors are typically motivated to give back to those in need.

- The fundraiser must lead by example. Prospective donors are much more likely to open their purse strings if the person asking for their money has done the same. I pledged $5 million to attract a star researcher to the Eye Institute, and then another $10 million to make it a major force for improving people's lives. I could hardly have asked others to give if I had not led by example.

- I'm always surprised how many donors don't understand the benefits of giving shares rather than cash, despite the removal of the capital gains tax on charitable donations of listed securities in the 2006 federal budget. This opportunity should be discussed with every prospective donor during the solicitation. There are two main benefits: first, when you give shares, the value is exempt from the capital gains tax that you would ultimately need to pay when you sell the shares in the future; second, the charitable donation tax credit can be used to reduce the income tax that you would otherwise pay on your cash income. Your after-tax cash income actually goes up as a result of a donation of shares.

- Encourage "smart giving." Rather than asking for a one-time donation, you are likely to get a far more generous response by suggesting a pledge spread over several years. Anyone donating shares that they expect to appreciate in value will be far more generous with a pledge over five years than a one-time donation. Also, explain to prospective donors the benefits of giving while they are alive, rather than a bequest in a will. By giving now, they will have the satisfaction of experiencing first-hand the impact their donation has on a favourite charity or non-profit. And I'll say this again, because seldom have truer words been spoken: "It's better to give it away with a warm hand than a cold hand. He who gives while he lives, also knows where it goes."

Any giving is better than none. While I naturally direct most of my donations to the charities where I am a board member, I receive requests from a long list of other groups.

Over the years, I have made or pledged donations to more than three hundred charities, mostly in Canada, because I knew the individual making the request, and it was for a good cause. These donations make up a modest proportion of the charities' needs, but they nonetheless give me great satisfaction. Serving on charity boards, too, has been a rich experience. It has opened my eyes to how crucial these organizations are to so many Canadians. It reminds me of how important it is to "pay forward" what we have received on our road to success.

BE AN AGENT FOR CHANGE

My campaign for a relaxation in Canada's tax rules relating to charitable donations has taught me some valuable lessons on lobbying for change in public policy. I've learned that anyone can be an advocate, and even a lobbyist. You have to keep at it with diligence and lots of hard work, but that's the only way change can happen:

- If you want to grab a politician's attention, send a personal "snail mail" letter. While e-mails are the simplest form of communication, MPs are swamped with e-mails and are unlikely to read many of them. They are much more likely to read a personal letter that is actually signed—not stamped with a signature—and mailed to their Ottawa office or their constituency office.
- Reach ALL the relevant people. There's no room for partisanship. It is essential to educate Members of Parliament and senators from all parties on your proposal. You need to outline why the proposal is relevant to voters in their communities and why it's good public policy *and* good politics.

All MPs need to hear your message, because you never know which party will form the next government, and whether it will be a majority or a minority. If it's a minority, you may need the support of every party, bar none.

- Engage leaders in every riding across Canada. MPs and senators listen to local business and community leaders, many of whom serve as volunteers and non-profit board members. Be sure to brief as many of these leaders as possible on the benefits of your proposal and ask them to meet with their local MPs; they need to tell the politicians how their own communities will benefit. And ask them to raise the issue at caucus meetings in Ottawa.

I believe you gain credibility by expanding your exposure in the philanthropic world, as I did. I became involved with my alma mater, Western University, as well as with the United Way and a hospital foundation, among others. Doing so meant that I could speak with authority and credibility to MPs, senators, and the federal finance committee.

THE IMPORTANCE OF GOOD HEALTH

My commitment to keeping physically and mentally fit has made one of the most valuable contributions to my happiness, longevity, and success. These are my secrets:

- Maintain a positive attitude, no matter how difficult the circumstances. I'm glad I read *The Power of Positive Thinking* as long ago as the 1960s, when I was still new to the business world. Since then, I've taken a "glass half full" view to every challenge I've encountered and to my leadership style. It makes it much easier to achieve success.

- Transcendental meditation has done wonders in improving my judgment and communication skills, and in my ability to make better decisions. I've been practising it faithfully twice a day for more than fifty years now. The investment of time has been well worthwhile. I believe TM deserves a much bigger role in our approach to mental health.

- The nature of the business world—long hours, lunch and dinner meetings, travel—makes it easy to overindulge, so I do my best to stay in shape. A healthy diet is key. To help keep me honest, I weigh myself daily on my bathroom scale; if there's even the smallest weight gain, I can nip it in the bud.

- Everyone should work at keeping their body in shape. To that end, never underestimate the value of a healthy diet and plenty of exercise. Having the discipline to follow this regimen, day in and day out, may be a challenge, but it is also very rewarding. For decades I was a runner, and nowadays I walk at least five thousand steps a day. Most weeks, I spend about an hour and a half on an elliptical trainer, and do Pilates and gym classes at least twice a week. I also see a personal trainer weekly. The result: I've been able to maintain the same weight throughout my adult life. Thomas Jefferson neatly sums up my approach to eating: "We seldom repent of having eaten too little."[58]

- "HBN: Horizontal by Nine" is my motto. Each night, I'm in bed no later than 9:30. Getting enough sleep, preferably eight to nine hours, gives me the energy to get through the busiest of days with a clear mind. I also make sure to draw up my next day's to-do list before I hit the sack. That way, I can relax as I drop off to sleep.

And finally, perhaps the most important lesson of all from the past eighty-four years: maintain a sense of humour. Making people laugh gives me a lot of satisfaction. Laughter not only relieves stress but also enhances your relationships. Laughing simply makes life more fun!

CHAPTER 10

SILVER LININGS IN TOUGH TIMES

A s the year 2020 dawned, I was confident that my work as an author was nearing an end. I had immersed myself in the fascinating world of publishers, editors, and fact-checkers for more than three years, and this book appeared to be all but done. We had gone through numerous versions of each chapter; names and dates had been carefully checked and double-checked; and Barlow Books' expert team of editors had, both literally and figuratively, crossed all the t's and dotted all the i's. *Lessons Learned* would soon be in the hands of the printers. We had even booked a room at the York Club in Toronto for the launch party, scheduled for Tuesday May 12. I was looking forward to a convivial evening in the company of well over 100 friends, family members, and business associates.

And then the world turned upside down, in more ways than one. Anna and I were enjoying our annual beach vacation at the Sandy Lane resort in warm and sunny Barbados when I first heard about the deadly new virus that was sweeping through the Chinese city of Wuhan. Like so many other North Americans, I didn't think much of it to start with, but within weeks of arriving home in Toronto, we found ourselves in lockdown. It didn't take long to realize that at least for the time being—and perhaps much longer—we would be leading very different lives from anything

I had experienced in my eighty-five years. Instead of going to the office from Monday to Friday, I found myself working at home seven days a week. The receptions, lunches, dinners, and other social events that I enjoyed so much were suddenly a thing of the past. Visits to the gym were out of the question. Social isolation became the name of the game.

But as the days and weeks wore on, I was surprised to find that the disruption also opened new horizons. "Crises create opportunities" has long been one of my favourite expressions, and COVID-19 has turned out to be no exception. That applies even to the writing of this book. To my great regret, the May 12 launch party was no longer in the cards and we had no choice but to delay publication of the book. The good news was that I would be able to add another chapter about my experiences during the pandemic and the lessons I learned from them. Sure enough, there has been no shortage of such lessons.

Many of my friends and acquaintances were not at all happy being confined to their homes, seven days a week. They missed going to the office, the club, and the gym. The changes in every-day routine demanded by social isolation and physical distancing were not easy. However, that was not my experience. As I told my three children in an e-mail in late April: "Working from home seven days a week has created a lot of opportunities and, this may surprise you, but I've been very happy working from home for the past several weeks." I added some smiley faces—☺ ☺ ☺—just to underscore my point and then spelled out some of the tangible benefits of my new routine:

■ A healthier lifestyle. As I discovered long ago, the four keys to a healthy lifestyle are exercise, diet and nutrition, sleep, and stress management. With no social or business commitments in the evening, being at home seven days a week, to my surprise and delight, enabled me to improve on all four counts.

Throughout the lockdown, I continued to work out on my elliptical trainer twice a week. Of course, my Pilates trainer was not able to come to the gym in person but, thanks to an iPad and FaceTime, she put me through all the same exercises on my reformer machine. What's more, I began taking a thirty-minute walk around the neighbourhood first thing each morning, something I never did pre-COVID. According to my Fitbit, I was taking 7,000 to 10,000 steps a day by April and May, almost double the number when I was going to the office.

The lockdown also helped improve my eating habits. Having breakfast, lunch, and dinner at home every day meant a much healthier diet. No more of those delicious but fattening and blood-clotting desserts that I used to eat in restaurants or at business events. Instead, I switched to healthy desserts, like a bowl of mixed berries every day after lunch, and occasionally a small slice of apple pie after dinner—but never with ice cream! The proof of the pudding—quite literally—was that I managed to lose three pounds between April and June.

On the sleep front, with no social or business commitments in the evening, I was able to adhere far more rigorously to my motto of *Horizontal by Nine*. Not only was I in bed by 9 p.m., but I was sleeping more soundly than I had in years.

Finally, isolation did wonders for my meditation routine. Before COVID, I would typically close the door of my downtown office half an hour before lunch or relax in the back seat of the car as my driver was taking me home in the afternoon.

It didn't take long to realize that neither of those settings was as comfortable as my home office chair, with the result that the quality of my meditation improved noticeably, making me feel more relaxed and ready for whatever else COVID-19 was about to throw at us.

All in all, I was in better health by the summer than I had been before the pandemic struck.

- A much cleaner and tidier home. For the first time in many, many years, I—with a lot of help from Remy, one of our housekeepers—cleaned all the drawers in my desk and the credenzas in my home office, as well as my dressing room, bedroom, and bathroom. It gave me a good deal of satisfaction to turf out a ton of papers and other stuff that I hadn't looked at in years and would never need in the future. We separated the remaining items into two groups: those for which I still had a use, and those I was unlikely to need, but someone else might find useful. The latter turned out to be a large pile of shirts, sweaters, trousers, shoes, and briefcases, among others. I gave my kids first option to pick out anything they might want, but on one condition: given the times we were living in, they would have to sift through the materials in the garden, rather than inside the house.

  This spring cleaning would never have happened if I had not been working at home seven days of the week. Seeing the garbage bags go out the door gave me almost as much satisfaction as closing a deal at the office.

- A different—and, in many ways, refreshing—social life. It came as a bit of a surprise to discover that physical isolation did not necessarily mean total isolation. Indeed, the time spent at home reinforced old friendships and even set the stage for a few new ones. For the first time in thirty-seven years, Anna and I had breakfast, lunch, and dinner together every day of the week. This was a real blessing because we had more time together that summer than any other in the previous 37 years. The lockdown also provided an opportunity to connect with our neighbours, some for the first time, as I ventured out for my morning walk. And what a pleasure it was. Back in the house, I gained a fresh appreciation for the fine job that our two housekeepers, Remy and Brigitte, do each and every day.

- You're never too old to learn something new. The lockdown turned out to be an excuse to explore some previously unfamiliar, but also exciting, technologies. I used Zoom for the first time to participate in board meetings of the four not-for-profit groups especially close to my heart—the Toronto General and Western Hospital Foundation; the advisory board of Western University's Ivey Business School; the major individual giving cabinet of the United Way of Toronto, Peel and York Region; and Business and the Arts. Zoom and conference calls have also been invaluable for board meetings of goeasy and Murchison Minerals, an exploration company of which I am an independent director. Zoom is certainly better than a telephone conference because you can see the participants' faces and expressions on the screen. But I definitely prefer in-person meetings and am looking forward to their return.

Last, but by no means least, I gained a much better understanding of how to get the most from my iPhone, iPad, and laptop. I learned how to use a number of iPhone features that

I had previously ignored and added several apps. I also bought a wireless printer, so I can now print documents sent from the iPhone—an especially useful device, given that I much prefer reading lengthy documents on paper rather than on a screen. Another addition to my home office was a shredder, enabling me to easily and quickly destroy confidential documents.

Whatever the silver linings of being cooped up at home, the spring and summer of 2020 also turned out to be a time of deep sorrow and, indeed, one of the toughest periods of my life. My older brother Paul passed away in mid-July at the age of ninety, leaving Cy as my only surviving sibling. Anna's sudden death exactly one month later was a devastating blow. We had been close companions for almost forty years, and many of my achievements would never have happened without her support and encouragement. Just two days before her death, we were dancing together in the garden to Neil Diamond singing "Sweet Caroline" as we celebrated our long friendship and marriage.

On a broader front, the pandemic has turned into a tragedy unimaginable when Anna and I returned from Barbados in January 2020. As I put the finishing touches to this chapter in October 2020, the death toll from COVID-19 had topped 10,000 in Canada and was approaching 230,000 in the US and had surpassed 1.1 million worldwide. In the US more people have died than were killed in the Vietnam and Korean wars combined. The cost has been equally high among the living, pushing unemployment up to levels not seen since the Great Depression of the 1930s, wiping out an uncountable number of small businesses and thrusting many households that appeared to be emerging into the middle class over the past decade or two back into poverty.

With the pandemic likely to widen rather than narrow economic and social inequalities, the role of philanthropy cannot be overstated. Almost every charity has seen a marked drop in revenues, with the result that many face significant financial challenges in carrying out their work. The privileged among us have an obligation to help them, providing another compelling argument for my campaign to persuade the federal government to remove the capital gains tax on charitable donations of private company shares and real estate.

To press my case, I wrote two open letters to MPs and senators, which were published by *Policy* magazine during the fall of 2020. I tried to underline the serious situation facing charities, and the urgent need for government action:

The economic and employment losses are indicative of an unprecedented emergency among charities. A May 2020 study by Imagine Canada reports donations declining by 31 percent, with 73 percent of charities seeing donations down. The report forecasts a loss of private sector donations of between $4.2 billion and $6.3 billion depending on the length of the crisis, with job losses estimated between 117,000 and 195,000.

This is devastating for the charitable sector, for the Canadians who provide these services, and the millions of Canadians who receive them. A report by the Cardus think tank in July found that seven charities out of 10 reported lower revenues and had already laid off 84,000 full and part-time workers.

Fortunately, there is something to be done for it, which would deliver immediate relief to help Canadians through the present economic emergency without significant additional costs to a fiscal framework that is already running historic deficits.

The proposal is simplicity itself, and achievable at low cost while significantly stimulating donations to the charitable sector.

The government would simply remove the capital gains tax on donations of private company shares and real estate to a registered charity. The foregone federal tax of $50-$60 million would result in an increase of charitable donations several times over. Existing jobs would be saved, new jobs would be created and urgently needed benefits would be delivered to Canadians.

This can be accomplished by a simple amendment to the Income Tax Act that could easily be adopted by Parliament either as a stand-alone measure or as part of a fiscal update expected during the fall sitting. As a tax change, it could be implemented immediately.

This is not a matter for partisan debate or division. Our soundings indicate that parties in the House would support such a measure, as would members of the Senate.

And all stakeholders in our hospitals, social service agencies, universities and the arts, and the millions of Canadians they serve, will be very appreciative of any additional support as a timely reminder that we are, indeed, all in this together.

It is estimated that this measure could stimulate an extra $200 million in donations to Canada's charities. As this book goes to press, it is my sincere hope that our long campaign will bear fruit in the 2021 budget.

■ ■ ■

After almost sixty years in the investment banking industry, I've lived through some major shocks in the stock market, including the Black Monday market crash on October 19, 1987, and the global financial crisis of 2007–08. However, the COVID-19 pandemic has had a far more profound impact on the global economy than any of the others. Who could have imagined that Canada's unemployment rate would jump from 5.2 per cent in January 2020 to over 13 per cent in April and May, with almost two million people out of work? The stock market has left us all dazed, with the Dow Jones index plummeting from an all-time record of almost 30,000 in February to under 20,000 a month later, and then staging a sharp but volatile recovery during the summer and early fall.

The scale of the turbulence really hit home to me as I watched the gyrations of goeasy, in which I am the largest single shareholder. goeasy stock reached an all-time high of $79.87 on Valentine's Day 2020, valuing the company at more than $1.1 billion. By late March, it had sunk to little more than $21. I'm pleased to say that the shares have recovered since then as investors have realized the potential of goeasy's business model at a time when many consumers are looking for some extra cash. What's more, Jason Mullins and his team took timely action to ensure that the business entered the crisis from a position of strength, and that it was well positioned to navigate the economic downturn. As of late October, the shares were trading at around $72, giving the company a market value of over a billion dollars. The rebound was a tribute to those precautionary measures, and I'm confident even better times lie ahead.

What lessons are investors to draw from these epic times? The one word that I share with anyone who asks that question is "uncertainty," whether it's about the timeline for a recovery in the global economy or the longer-term impacts of the pandemic on Canada and the rest of the world. The clouded outlook has been compounded by the failure of governments around the world to collaborate in the fight against the virus, with the result that we lack one of the prerequisites for tackling a crisis of this magnitude, namely, a coherent international strategy.

My friend David Ingram, who played such a big role in goeasy's success, summed up the sad state of affairs in an e-mail at the height of the pandemic in May 2020:

> I think you can basically boil the world into three strategic approaches. On one extreme, you have China that went into a targeted full lockdown with a clear set of rules and strict authority for isolation that kept the virus from any chance of spreading. The Chinese used technology such as phone signals for contact tracing, regarding privacy as a secondary priority to managing public health risks. Many other Asian countries learned from the SARS crisis in 2003 and H1N1 in 2009, when China was also an early transmitter. Culturally, Asians tend to comply more willingly than North Americans with rules set by their governments, and they are more considerate towards each other. They have worn masks to prevent spreading a virus long before such measures were recommended or required.
>
> On the other extreme, Sweden did not choose a lockdown as it had a strategy to pursue herd immunity, allowing large parts of the population to be infected. The Swedes were

well aware that many people would show no symptoms, and that death rates would be quite high only in a few specific groups, notably those older than 70, people with pre-existing respiratory diseases and in generally poor health, and residents of long-term care homes. In line with their culture of a social contract, they tend to voluntarily follow principle. In line with that approach, guidelines such as social distancing and hygiene were communicated but not enforced. Most businesses were allowed to stay open, co-existing with the new virus rather than declaring war on it. The death rate in Sweden as a ratio of the total population has remained lower than the U.K. and U.S. As scientists believe 70% of the population need to be infected to reach herd immunity, it will take time to tell if this approach is successful. It's also important to understand that Swedes have the advantage of a strong health care system that is fully government funded. The obesity rate in Sweden is just 13% against 40% in the U.S. so in some ways you have a different starting point that informs your strategy.

Finally, you have the U.S. approach which boils down to NO strategy. The U.S. detected COVID-19 before it exploded in the country, but didn't move to stop it as it entered New York from Europe. President Trump decided that the economy needed to open despite some states not reaching their peak rates of infection, and despite a very low rate of testing for the size of population. He abdicated responsibility, leaving it to each state to decide when it should reopen and what restrictions should be put in place. Subjected to a barrage of polarized information, Americans began to question their trust in the government and health agencies' ability to make decisions based on science and not on political expediency. A lack of mask enforcement, looser controls on social distancing, demographic differences such as low single-family occupancy (28% versus 50% in Sweden) and less social contracting than other cultures all mean that the U.S. requires a more rigorous national governance and compliance charter for containing the virus. Given that domestic travel was not restricted in the U.S., the risk of a second wave before a vaccine was available was bound to be greater than in many other parts of the world. Canada potentially falls into the same category, as provincial leaders rather than the federal government make these decisions. What gives Canadians a better chance of success is its universal health care system, more centrist political agenda and a population that is less divided and more supportive of community. Plus, Canada has the advantage of the world's second largest land mass, so less population density.

One result of this divided and disappointing response has been a sense of heightened unpredictability, raising the question: What should investors do? My advice has been blunt and simple: Be patient.

While I have never been a portfolio manager, my investment strategy has always been to focus on a few companies that meet my investment criteria, and to invest for the long term, no matter how wild the swings in the market. That philosophy has not changed since March 2020. I still like companies headed by a chief executive with unquestioned integrity and a vision for the firm to be a leader in its industry. The CEO must be an effective team builder with a strong drive to succeed. The business should have a tangible advantage over its competitors, preferably in an industry that has high barriers to entry. A company possessing these attributes will, I believe, prosper through thick and thin.

goeasy is a good example. From my very first investment, I have ignored market fluctuations, and that approach has paid off handsomely. goeasy shares hit a low of just $5 during the 2008 financial crisis, but they have staged an impressive recovery. Even the COVID-19 low of $21 in March 2020 represented a quadrupling over twelve years, and the impressive bounce-back during the spring and summer more than vindicated my investment strategy.

Patience is the key. The pandemic will not last forever. As it subsides, companies will have an opportunity to refinance. My advice would be for them to do so as soon as financial markets permit. Those that strengthen their balance sheets will be in a formidable position to take advantage of future opportunities and absorb future shocks. Their shareholders will eventually reap handsome rewards.

Even so, my tolerance for risk is not infinite. Not long ago, one of my favourite expressions was "I can't sleep at night unless I am fully margined." But the recent turbulence on financial markets has undoubtedly made me more wary. I would now put it somewhat differently: "I can't sleep at night if I have any margin loans." Going one step further, a good friend convinced me that anyone can survive even the worst financial crisis, provided they have no debt.

The pandemic has been a stressful time for people from every walk of life—investors, workers, small business owners, and politicians. We owe a special debt of gratitude to the brave men and women on the front lines of the health-care system and to those who keep our supply chains running, whether it's picking fruit and vegetables on our farms, keeping supermarket shelves stocked, or delivering takeout meals.

Make no mistake, as I write this in October 2020, I am looking forward to the day when normal life resumes. It will feel good to head downtown again each morning. I'll be glad to see my gym instructor in person and to meet friends and business associates over lunch and dinner. Less volatility in the stock market will be welcome. Not least, I'm looking forward to setting a new date for that York Club book launch! My one regret is that Anna will not be at my side.

ACKNOWLEDGEMENTS

I'd like to thank the great members of the Barlow Books team, who have been extremely helpful to me in writing this book. These include my two editors, Bernard Simon and Bonnie Munday; fact-checker Sarah Reid; publisher Sarah Scott; managing editor-at-large Tracy Bordian; and copy editor Eleanor Gasparik. Each of these people has given me great suggestions on a very timely basis. In fact, without their support and advice, I'm not sure this book would have made it to print! In addition, I thank Cat Nadeau, my executive assistant, and Debby de Groot, my publicist.

NOTES

[1] Calvin Coolidge, "Favourite Calvin Coolidge Quotes," Forbes Library, comment from Calvin Coolidge Presidential Library and Museum, May 26, 2009, accessed January 17, 2020, https://forbeslibrary.org/blog/2008/12/10/favorite-calvin-coolidge-quotes/.

[2] Jim Clifton, "The World's Broken Workplace," Gallup, June 13, 2017, accessed January 17, 2020, https://news.gallup.com/opinion/chairman/212045/world-broken-workplace.aspx?g_source=position1&g_medium=related&g_campaign=tiles.

[3] Warren Buffett, letter to Donald Johnson, September 26, 2015.

[4] Donald Johnson, e-mail to Debbie Bosanek, assistant to Warren Buffett, June 9, 2017.

[5] Ibid.

[6] Donald Johnson, e-mail to Debbie Bosanek, assistant to Warren Buffett, June 12, 2017.

[7] Debbie Bosanek, assistant to Warren Buffett, e-mail to Donald Johnson, July 17, 2017.

[8] Debbie Bosanek, assistant to Warren Buffett, e-mail to Donald Johnson, August 10, 2017.

[9] Jacques Ménard, e-mail to Sarah Reid, researcher on behalf of author, July 9, 2019.

[10] Barry Cooper, phone interview with Sarah Reid, researcher on behalf of author, July 10, 2019.

[11] Ibid.

[12] Peter Eby, confirmed in interview with Sarah Reid, researcher on behalf of author, July 10, 2019.

[13] Roger Lomax, e-mail to Sarah Reid, researcher on behalf of author, July 19, 2019.

[14] Anthony Depalma, "Canada, for now, Rejects Two Large Bank Mergers," New York Times, December 15, 1998, accessed January 17, 2020, www.nytimes.com/1998/12/15/business/international-business-canada-for-now-rejects-two-large-bank-mergers.html.

[15] Roger Lomax, e-mail to Sarah Reid, researcher on behalf of author, July 27, 2019.

[16] Ibid.

[17] David Yeilding, e-mail to Sarah Reid, researcher on behalf of author, July 14, 2019.

[18] Conrad Black, confirmed by e-mail to Sarah Reid, researcher on behalf of author, July 4, 2019.

[19] "Donald K. Johnson Eye Institute," University Health Network Krembil Neuroscience Centre, accessed January 17, 2020, www.uhn.ca/KNC/Pages/Donald-K_Johnson_Eye_Institute.aspx?utm_source=https://www.uhn.ca/knc/patientsfamilies/pages/donald-k_johnson_eye_institute.aspx&utm_medium=404&utm_campaign=redirects.

[20] Allan Slomovic, e-mail to Sarah Reid, researcher on behalf of author, July 12, 2019.

[21] "Chapter 3: Budget Recommendations," House of Commons Committee on Finance, 1996, accessed January 17, 2020, www.ourcommons.ca/Content/Archives/Committee/352/fine/reports/05_1996-12/chap3-e.html.

[22] "Budget Plan, Including Supplementary Information and Notices of Ways and Means Motions," Department of Finance, February 18, 1997, accessed January 17, 2020, http://publications.gc.ca/Pilot/Finance/Budget97/bp97-e.pdf.

[23] Ross McGregor, e-mail to Sarah Reid, researcher on behalf of author, June 24, 2019.

[24] Bob Rae, e-mail to Sarah Reid, researcher on behalf of author, July 7, 2019.

[25] "Stand Up for Canada: Conservative Party of Canada Federal Election Platform 2006," Conservative Party of Canada, accessed January 20, 2020, www.poltext.org/sites/poltext.org/files/plateformesV2/Canada/CAN_PL_2006_PC_en.pdf.

[26] "Finance Minister Announces New Measures to Support Charitable Giving," Department of Finance Canada, January 22, 2006, accessed January 17, 2020, www.collectionscanada.gc.ca/eppp-archive/100/205/300/liberal-ef/06-01-22/www.liberal.ca/print_e.aspx@id=11422.

[27] Andrew Willis, "Don Johnson, 2007" *The Globe and Mail*, November 17, 2009, www.theglobeandmail.com/news/national/don-johnson-2007/article4292732/.

[28] Donald Johnson, "Liberals Should Reconsider this Capital-Gains Oversight on Donations," *The Globe and Mail*, April 21, 2016, accessed January 17, 2020, www.theglobeandmail.com/report-on-business/rob-commentary/liberals-should-reconsider-this-capital-gains-oversight-on-donations/article29696147/.

[29] Marnie Spears, e-mail to Sarah Reid, researcher on behalf of author, June 28, 2019.

[30] Ivana Buric et al., "What Is the Molecular Signature of Mind-Body Interventions? A Systematic Review of Gene Expression Changes Induced by Meditation and Related Practices," *Frontiers in Immunology*, June 16, 2017, accessed January 20, 2020, www.frontiersin.org/articles/10.3389/fimmu.2017.00670/full.

[31] "Relaxation Techniques: Try these Steps to Reduce Stress," Mayo Clinic, April 19, 2017, accessed January 17, 2020, www.mayoclinic.org/healthy-lifestyle/stress-management/in-depth/relaxation-technique/art-20045368.

[32] "Transcendental Meditation for Anxiety," Maharishi Foundation USA, accessed January 17, 2020, www.tm.org/anxiety.

[33] Mario Orsatti, "New Studies Show Reduced Depression with Transcendental Meditation," TM Blog, August 3, 2010, accessed January 17, 2020, www.tm.org/blog/meditation/reduced-depression-transcendental-meditation/.

[34] Laura A. Pratt et al., "Antidepressant Use among Persons Aged 12 and Over: United States 2011–2014," NCHS Data Brief No. 283, Centres for Disease Control and Prevention, August 2017, accessed January 20, 2020, www.cdc.gov/nchs/products/databriefs/db283.htm.

[35] "Exercise and Immunity," MedlinePlus, US National Library of Medicine, accessed January 17, 2020, https://medlineplus.gov/ency/article/007165.htm.

[36] "Benefits of Exercise," MedlinePlus, US National Library of Medicine, accessed January 17, 2020, https://medlineplus.gov/benefitsofexercise.html.

[37] Ibid.

[38] Shashi K. Agarwal, "Cardiovascular Benefits of Exercise," *International Journal of General Medicine* (June 2012): 541–545, accessed January 17, 2020, www.ncbi.nlm.nih.gov/pmc/articles/PMC3396114/.

[39] "Exercising to Prevent a Stroke," HealthLinkBC, November 5, 2019, accessed January 20, 2020, www.healthlinkbc.ca/health-topics/hw223366.

[40] K.M. Diaz and D. Shimbo, "Physical Activity and the Prevention of Hypertension," Current Hypertension Reports (2013) 15: 659. https://doi.org/10.1007/s11906-013-0386-8.

[41] "Alzheimer's Disease: Can Exercise Prevent Memory Loss?" Mayo Clinic, April 20, 2019, accessed January 20, 2020, www.mayoclinic.org/diseases-conditions/alzheimers-disease/expert-answers/alzheimers-disease/faq-20057881.

[42] "Health Benefits of Physical Activity," HealthLinkBC, November 2016, accessed January 20, 2020, www.healthlinkbc.ca/physical-activity/health-benefits.

[43] Ibid.

[44] "Exercise and Your Arteries," Harvard Health Publishing, updated June 21, 2019, www.health.harvard.edu/heart-health/exercise_and_your_arteries.

[45] "Top 5 Lifestyle Changes to Improve Your Cholesterol," Mayo Clinic, August 11, 2018, accessed January 20, 2020, www.mayoclinic.org/diseases-conditions/high-blood-cholesterol/in-depth/reduce-cholesterol/art-20045935.

[46] "Depression and Anxiety: Exercise Eases Symptoms," Mayo Clinic, September 27, 2017, accessed January 20, 2020, www.mayoclinic.org/diseases-conditions/depression/in-depth/depression-and-exercise/art-20046495.

[47] Roberto Manfredini et al., "Daylight Saving Time, Circadian Rhythm, and Cardiovascular

Health," *Internal and Emergency Medicine* (2018) 13: 641. https://doi.org/10.1007/s11739-018-1900-4.

[48] "Could Daylight Saving Time Increase Heart Attack Risk?" *News Medical*, May 16, 2019, www.news-medical.net/whitepaper/20190516/Could-Daylight-Saving-Time-Increase-Heart-Attack-Risk.aspx.

[49] "Daylight Savings Time and Traffic Accidents," *The New England Journal of Medicine*, April 4, 1996, accessed January 17, 2020, www.medicine.mcgill.ca/epidemiology/hanley/communicationCommunication Communication/nejm199604043341416.pdf.

[50] Stanley Coren, *Sleep Thieves: An Eye-Opening Exploration into the Science and Mysteries of Sleep* (Toronto: Simon & Schuster, 1996). (Statement confirmed by Stanley Coren in e-mail to Sarah Reid, researcher on behalf of author, June 27, 2019.)

[51] Roberto Manfredini et al., "Daylight Saving Time, Circadian Rhythm, and Cardiovascular Health," *Internal and Emergency Medicine* (2018) 13: 641. https://doi.org/10.1007/s11739-018-1900-4.

[52] Norman Vincent Peale, *The Power of Positive Thinking* (New York: Prentice Hall, 1952).

[53] "Economic Moat," Investopedia, accessed 17 January 2020, www.investopedia.com/terms/e/economicmoat.asp.

[54] Winston Churchill, "Never Give In," speech delivered October 29, 1941, to the Harrow School, International Churchill Society, accessed January 17, 2020, https://winstonchurchill.org/resources/speeches/1941-1945-war-leader/never-give-in/.

[55] Plaque originally belonged to Robert Woodruff, who became president of the Coca-Cola Company in 1923. Robert Woodruff Foundation, accessed January 17, 2020, http://woodruff.org/about/robert-w-woodruff/.

[56] Thomas Jefferson, *Jefferson's Ten Rules ... Printed for Free Distribution by the Brooklyn Eagle Book, Job and Pamphlet Printing Department* [n.d.] (Brooklyn: N.p., 1900), accessed January 17, 2020, www.loc.gov/item/rbpe.13400400/.

[57] "Donald K. Johnson Eye Institute," *University Health Network Krembil Neuroscience Centre*, accessed January 17, 2020, www.uhn.ca/KNC/Pages/Donald-K_Johnson_Eye_Institute.aspx?utm_source=https://www.uhn.ca/knc/patientsfamilies/pages/donald-k_johnson_eye_institute.aspx&utm_medium=404&utm_campaign=redirects.

[58] Thomas Jefferson, *Jefferson's Ten Rules ... Printed for Free Distribution by the Brooklyn Eagle Book, Job and Pamphlet Printing Department* [n.d.] (Brooklyn: N.p., 1900), accessed January 17, 2020, www.loc.gov/item/rbpe.13400400/.

INDEX

Note: DJ = Donald Johnson